HAITI
THE BLACK SHEEP?

Why Foreign Aid Has Failed in Haiti
and What To Do About It

D1595754

CLAUDIA CHARLOT

Haiti: The Black Sheep?

Trilogy Christian Publishers A Wholly Owned Subsidiary of Trinity Broadcasting Network

2442 Michelle Drive Tustin, CA 92780

Unless otherwise indicated, all Scripture quotations are taken from the New International Version (NIV). Public domain. Scripture quotations marked ESV are taken from the ESV® Bible (The Holy Bible, English Standard Version®), copyright © 2001 by Crossway Bibles, a publishing ministry of Good News Publishers. Used by permission. All rights reserved. Scripture quotations marked NKJV are taken from the New King James Version®. Copyright © 1982 by Thomas Nelson. Used by permission. All rights reserved.

Rights Department, 2442 Michelle Drive, Tustin, CA 92780.

Trilogy Christian Publishing/TBN and colophon are trademarks of Trinity Broadcasting Network.

Cover design by: Grant Swank

For information about special discounts for bulk purchases, please contact Trilogy Christian Publishing.

Trilogy Disclaimer: The views and content expressed in this book are those of the author and may not necessarily reflect the views and doctrine of Trilogy Christian Publishing or the Trinity Broadcasting Network.

Manufactured in the United States of America

10 9 8 7 6 5 4 3 2 1

Library of Congress Cataloging-in-Publication Data is available.

ISBN: 978-1-68556-561-9

E-ISBN: 978-1-68556-562-6

To my husband, Guenson,
through whom I fell in love with the Haitian people.

There shall come a time
When these children in rags
Who litter the streets
Who know the crushing mastery of poverty
And the curses of dirt and slovenliness
Shall walk with heads erect
Proud owners of a new world
Masters of themselves
Admitting no inequality
Feeling no inferiority
Only a great humility and wonder
For the destiny that shall be theirs.

Jamaican poet H. D. Carberry (1921-1989)

ENDORSEMENTS

Haiti: The Black Sheep? is a book that brings hope to Haiti and to any person facing first-hand the challenges of long-term, systematic poverty in any part of the world. It reads like a novel with Claudia Charlot serving as a first-person narrator unweaving the personal story of her home nation, drawing the reader into a vivid world of harsh reality, hope, and faith. The writing is clear with insightful big picture perspectives brought to life with details and impeccable research. The writing is efficient in analysis and emotionally engaging in stories. If there is one book to read to learn to love, understand, cry alongside and celebrate Haiti, *Haiti: The Black Sheep?* is it.

—Dr. Brad Smith
President, Bakke Graduate University

This is a must-read to dispel all the disparaging thinking and remarks made about Haiti. The writing is compelling, covering history, culture, current-day issues and their interconnectedness. The research, especially regarding Federal Aid and NGOs, is sophisticated with the latest data. The conclusions are well thought through and give hope for Haiti. This book needs to be read by all people connected with Haiti, including the NGO sector, government, both local and international, people connected with the various church denominations and groups, both local and international. It is in this context a new Haiti can be reimagined.

—Jo Ann Lyon
Founder, World Hope International; former General
superintendent, The Wesleyan Church

My sincere congratulations to Dr. Claudia Charlot for the fine research job done in her book *Haiti: The Black Sheep?* Her extensive research reveals what is keeping Haiti so poor after 218 years of being the very first Free Black Republic of the world.

Her main focus is the way that foreign aid is perceived and handled both by those disbursing and receiving aid. She gives some very wise suggestions on how foreign aid can be used more effectively in Haiti. Her work is coming at a time when Haiti is facing major political, social, humanitarian, and economic crises. I wish that this wonderful work can be translated into French and Haitian Creole soon so that Haitian young people can be informed and encouraged to participate actively in reviving our beloved nation, Haiti.

May her fine work wake up our leaders, churches, and especially the youth to fight for a renewed Haitian society.

—Dr. Jules Casseus
Founder and consultant, Northern Haiti Christian University

Recent stories have reinforced in many Western minds the perceptions powerful media sources continue to hammer home: Haiti is hopeless and helpless. Corruption, political unrest, violence, and poverty are all highlighted to reinforce this message.

But are the people of Haiti really hopeless and helpless? Dr. Charlot leads her readers on a journey to a hope-filled understanding. Included is rich, wise advice on not only how outsiders should view Haiti with hopeful eyes, but also practical advice for building hope in the hearts of Haitians. Living in Haiti and working to develop next-generation Haitian leaders is Dr. Charlot's calling, and she and her husband are doing this with excellence at Emmaus University. I joyfully commend this book and Dr. Charlot as a hope-builder, equipping Haitians to build hope and urging outsiders to offer help that engages, involves, and empowers Haitians on their hope-building journeys, even enabling them to see themselves and their future through an essential lens of hope!

—Dr. Robert Fetherlin
President, One Mission Society Global

In the eyes of many, Haiti is a hopeless case. They explain its hopelessness on the assumptions that the help it receives to take it out of its condition is typically squandered through corruption, and that its people have no confidence in their own ability to build a prosperous nation. Dr. Charlot's book debunks both assumptions. Through qualitative and quantitative research, she shows that the misuse of the "aid" given to Haiti lies mostly elsewhere than in Haitian corruption, and that most Haitians have a positive attitude about the future of their land. She suggests that those who really want to help the country should gear their aid to unlock the agency of the Haitian people, and so doing, empower them to accomplish this task themselves. This book makes an important contribution to the challenge of Haiti's development. I recommend it highly.

—Dieumeme Noelliste, Ph.D.
Professor of Theological Ethics, Denver Seminary

Haiti, known as the poorest country in the Western Hemisphere, has become a mecca for short-term mission teams from the United States, 560 registered NGOs, multilateral donor agencies, and many others, all trying to "do good." But have they? In this theoretically grounded, well-researched, and riveting narrative, Claudia Charlot explores the legacy of years of paternalistic foreign aid poured into Haiti and uncovers the roots of dependency and the psychological impact this has had on many Haitians. This study does not blame the victims, which is so common, nor resigns to the endemic poverty, crime, and political instability. Rather, it champions biblical and kingdom-oriented hope and concludes with excellent recommendations. This is a great study with global implications and theological significance, and I recommend it highly.

—Dr. Darrell Whiteman
Anthropologist, Global Development

Dr. Claudia Charlot offers a straightforward, transparent look at "why foreign aid has failed in Haiti and what to do about it." Her work is filled with compelling research findings—spanning the physical, psychological, spiritual, and relational dimensions of life in Haiti.

In her new book, Dr. Charlot combines scholarly research with fascinating contextual illustrations. Her multi-pronged approach provides practical and doable solutions for the unique challenges faced in the lives of Haitians. She confronts tough situations where life does not make sense, yet God comes through, even in seemingly impossible situations. She believes that attitude is truly a difference-maker, and sometimes God works in ways never imagined. I endorse it enthusiastically with much appreciation for the author's insights.

—Dr. Wil Chevalier
Founder, LifeBranch Institute Intl.

In this important book *Haiti: The Black Sheep?* Claudia Charlot carefully examines different phenomena in the Haitian society, including Haitian history, culture, economy, and the religious experience of the Haitian people through the lens of Haiti's journey toward development. In particular, the author gives special attention to the intersection of foreign aid, donors, and the perceptions of recipients. The author argues that various perceptions of foreign aid, both from foreign donors and Haitian natives, affect the effectiveness of foreign aid interventions in the Caribbean country. The author, who remains optimistic about Haiti's future, recommends some practical and effective ways for the use of foreign aid in Haiti and to strengthen mutual rapport between Haitians and foreigners. I highly recommend this book to anyone who has an interest in Haitian history and the future economic development of the Haitian people and the country.

—Celucien L. Joseph, Ph.D.
Author of *Thinking in Public: Faith, Secular Humanism and Development in Jacques Roumain*

CLAUDIA CHARLOT

In her new book *Haiti: The Black Sheep?* Claudia Charlot provides a vivid description of Haitian history, modern culture, and a hope for what is possible in the future. She gives context for the consequences of past good intentions and clarity around what is needed most for true transformation to happen.

—Tami Heim
President and CEO, Christian Leadership Alliance

Claudia advocates for a model of active participation and self-sustainability, where the people of Haiti are recognized as energetic, capable, and innovative. I am grateful for Claudia for sustained excellence in shining light on this important topic. Her engaging work brings the true reality of human development in Haiti to the forefront.

—Shirley V. Hoogstra, J. D.
President, Council for Christian Colleges & Universities

ACKNOWLEDGEMENTS

I would like to thank all those who cheered me on as I completed this manuscript. Especially Dr. Ray Easley, my dissertation second reader, who gave me extensive feedback and was the first person to encourage me to have my dissertation published. Even though he passed away before seeing the completed project, his legacy lives on through this book.

Special thanks also to Dr. Darrell Whiteman, whose suggestions helped me to transform my dissertation into a more reader-friendly document.

Thanks also to everyone who took the time to read and endorse my book.

Table of Contents

INTRODUCTION..17

CHAPTER 1: POVERTY PARADOX...............................21

"Land of High Mountains"..22

Economy...24

The Haitian Diaspora..24

Natural Disasters...25

Politics..26

CHAPTER 2: HAITIAN CULTURE..............................27

Chicken!...29

Worldview..30

Animism...31

Voodoo and Healing..33

CHAPTER 3: WITCHCRAFT AND FOREIGN AID...................37

Judge Not...40

CHAPTER 4: Patron-Client Culture.............................43

CHAPTER 5: HAITI'S COLONIAL PAST......................47

"Pearl of the Antilles"...47

Slavery and Battle of Independence.................................48

The Price of Freedom...51

New Oppressors 52

The American Occupations 53

The Duvalier Legacy 56

CHAPTER 6: WESTERN MEDIA AND FOREIGN AID 59

Haiti Stigmatized by Western Media 59

Western Media and Haiti's Economic Decline 60

Media Coverage of the 2010 Earthquake 61

Media Portrayal of Disease in Haiti 62

Media Portrayal of Violence in Haiti 65

Media Portrayal of Kidnappings in Haiti 68

Media Portrayal of Political Instability in Haiti 71

"An Exceptional Haiti" 72

Media Madness 72

CHAPTER 7: Foreign Aid in Haiti 77

Instrumental Philanthropy 77

US Aid and Haitian Politics 79

Food Aid 80

Foreign Aid as an Engine of Development 83

CHAPTER 8: Foreign Aid after the 2010 Earthquake 85

Where Did All the Money Go? 85

Haitian Government Bypassed 86

CHAPTER 9: REPUBLIC OF NGOs..89

Multilateral Aid..89

Lack of NGO Accountability...90

Managing Poverty..91

Haitian Perceptions of NGOs..93

Disaster Tourism...94

CHAPTER 10: EMPIRICAL RESEARCH...............................97

Description of Research Results..98

Group 1: "Die-Hard Optimists"...99

Group 2: "Die-Hard Patriots"..103

Group 3: "Die-Hard Foreign Aid Advocates"...................106

A Missing Group: The "Die-Hard Pessimists"...................107

CHAPTER 11: INTERPRETATION OF
RESEARCH RESULTS..111

How Do Haitians Perceive Foreign Aid?..........................111

How Do Haitians Perceive Foreign Aid Donors?.............112

How Do Haitians Perceive Themselves?...........................113

How Does Receiving Foreign Aid Affect Self-Efficacy
and Work Ethic in Haiti?..114

CHAPTER 12: SYMPOSIUM..119

Survey 1: Main Reasons Why Haiti Is Underdeveloped......119

Survey 2: Choose One of the Three Factors 120

Group Discussions 121

CHAPTER 13: GET YOUR HEAD IN THE GAME! 125

Deficit-Based Community Development 126

Unhealthy Dependency 128

Avoid Paternalism 128

Actively Involve Aid Recipients 129

Rethink Haiti 131

Relief vs. Development 132

CHAPTER 14: HEALTHY AID 135

Academics and Skills Training 135

Business Training and Micro-Finance 138

Environmental Programs 140

Mentorship 142

CHAPTER 15: PERCEPTION AND PROPHECY 145

What Is a Blessing? 145

Sticks and Stones... 146

Perceptions and Parenting 148

Perceptions and Politics 149

Prophetic Leadership 150

CHAPTER 16: WORLDVIEW TRANSFORMATION 153

Racial Reconciliation...153

Worldview Transformation..155

Demons of Poverty..155

Spiritual Warfare...157

Weh Unnu Nuh Leffi People Dem Alone?......................................158

CARRY ON...161

APPENDICES...163

Appendix 1: COVID Death Rate for Selected Caribbean Countries....163

Appendix 2: Q Set..164

Appendix 3: Score Sheet..167

Appendix 4: A Completed Game Board...168

NOTES...169

INTRODUCTION

Two Sisters Flipped a Coin, One of Them Was Sent to Hell[1]

So reads a headline describing the immigration crisis involving thousands of mostly Haitian immigrants camped at the US-Mexico border in September 2021. One sister stayed in Mexico while the other was deported back to Haiti. How did "hell" become an acceptable term for prominent news outlets to use to refer to Haiti? How did this perception of Haiti become so widespread that Western media houses feel at liberty to use such a term to dehumanize Haitians and demonize poverty while no one hardly blinks an eye at such denigration? "Hell" is not only the worst place to live but also the only place beyond remedy. Is Haiti really the worst country on earth?

The goal of this book is to examine how foreign aid donors view Haitians, how Haitians view foreign aid donors and themselves and how these perceptions affect the effectiveness of foreign aid interventions in Haiti. I will also present and discuss the findings of my doctoral research and make suggestions about how foreign aid can be used more effectively in Haiti.

Haiti has been dubbed "the Republic of NGOs"[2] because of its large number of non-governmental organizations (NGOs) yet remains mired in poverty. Throughout the 20th century but especially after the devastating earthquake in 2010, Haiti has received copious amounts of foreign aid—$13 billion to be exact.[3] It is assumed that foreign aid exists to mitigate against the negative circumstances a developing country faces that cause it to be mired in poverty. However, this does not appear to be the case in Haiti.

Two hundred sixteen years after its triumphant emergence as the world's first free Black republic,[4] Haiti's key human development indicators remain weak, and it continues to experience economic growth rates below that of other developing countries in the region.[5] This conundrum begs the question: "Why does Haiti remain poor and underdeveloped despite receiving large amounts of foreign aid?"

When I moved to Haiti with my husband, Guenson, after the devastating earthquake in 2010, I found it a curious contradiction to be called *blan* (white) by the locals. I soon realized that this term is laden with a lot of signification, such as "a wealthy, resourceful foreigner," "the CIA," "former colonizers," and "people trying to exploit the country's wealth." This label was disturbing for me, a Black woman from Jamaica, a proudly Black nation, which is also a former slave colony. I later learned the origin of the label "blan." After Jean Jacques Dessalines led Haiti to victory over the French, "to solve the problem of racial identity" and unite all Haitians, he declared that all citizens "would be referred to as black."[6] So by default, all foreigners were considered "white." Thankfully, as I acquired the language and immersed in the culture through thick and thin, I slowly became more accepted and trusted. However, Haitians' general suspicion of foreigners caused me to wonder what the root cause was and what impact it has on foreign aid projects and economic development overall in a country so aid-dependent.

It was also a mystery to me how people in Haiti survived when so many loitered on the streets every day without gainful employment. I soon learned that Haiti's communal culture is many people's social security net. "You feed me today, and I'll feed you tomorrow" is the unstated mantra in Haiti's social contract. Apart from remittances, foreign aid is the single largest source of Haiti's income and survival.[7] Haiti's unemployment rate remains perpetually high, with over half the population unemployed or underemployed. In developed economies, it is taken for granted that a vibrant small business sector is the key to job creation, economic growth, and general human flourishing. Yet, when most missionaries and NGOs from North America and Europe come to Haiti, the knee-jerk reaction is relief projects despite Haiti's daunting double-digit unemployment rate. This observation made me interested in the impact of foreign aid on Haiti's economic development. Does endemic poverty in Haiti perpetuate high levels of foreign aid or the other way around?

CHAPTER 1: POVERTY PARADOX

"Piti piti, zwazo fè nich" (Little by little, the bird makes its nest).
—Don't give up.

Most people know that Haiti is the poorest country in the western hemisphere, with 80 percent of its population living under the poverty line and 54 percent in abject poverty.[8] What many people do not know is Haiti's poverty paradox.

Guenson and I moved to Haiti on blind faith in August 2010. With no home church or sending organization, no clue where we would live, and $1700 to our name, we packed our belongings and started shipping them to Cap-Haitian. Thankfully, a Sunday school class from Christ United Methodist Church in Jackson, Mississippi, generously paid our shipping costs and our rent when we found a place at the last minute. With no job prospects and Guenson working about $300 a month at a small Bible school, we decided to start an English school with half our savings. It took off and sustained us for five years, in addition to funding our church plant and helping us help countless others.

At the same time, we lived next door to a young man who was unemployed. He was a devout Christian who had moved from the countryside to Cap-Haitian seeking a better life, but evidently, things did not turn out as planned. He depended on his family overseas to send him money to get by. Eventually, his brother decided to send him a lumpsum of $3000 so that he could start a small business and not have to depend on him every month. He came to Guenson to share the good news and to ask him for advice. We both were impressed by the brother's gift—no one had ever handed us $3000 before! We suggested that he buy phone minutes wholesale to sell, but he thought that was below him. After all, he was a "Philosopher"—the grand title given to the distinguished few who manage to finish high school in Haiti. We discussed other options. We did not hear much from him until some time later when he came to explain to us the difficult situation he was in and asked whether we could help him with some food. We were puzzled, to say the least! "What happened to the money you got not too long ago?" He explained that by the time family members got wind of the news, and after spending a little here and there, the money disappeared, and he was back where he started.

Over the years, we have heard countless stories like this. We have also seen so many people spend thousands of American dollars to pay for passage on makeshift boats or to pay bogus travel agents to escape to the United States, Canada, South America—anywhere. We often reflect on how much that money could have done if put to good use. Many Haitians are rich yet poor.

"Land of High Mountains"

The island Haiti shares with the Dominican Republic was named Quisqueya, "Mother of the Earth," by its indigenous Taino inhabitants.[9] Christopher Columbus arrived in Haiti on December 6, 1492, and named the island Hispaniola, "little Spain." After a large settlement of French settlers seeking gold overwhelmed the Spanish, Spain ceded 27,560 sq. km. of land in the western one-third of the island to the French in the 1697 Treaty of Ryswick.[10] This part of the country was later renamed Haiti, another name the indigenous Indians had given to the island, which means "land of high mountains." Haiti became the first free Black Republic in the world when it won its independence from France in 1804.[11] "History has witnessed many insurrections and revolutions, but only one nation has emerged from a slave uprising: the Republic of Haiti."[12]

Most of the gruesome international stories that tabloids feature are based in the capital, Port-au-Prince, home to roughly two million[13] of Haiti's 11.3 million people[14] (See Figure 1 for map of Haiti[15]). The capital is often turbulent in an otherwise peaceful country. Haiti has the second youngest population in the region, with 55 percent of its citizens being under age of twenty-four.[16]

Figure 1: Map of Haiti

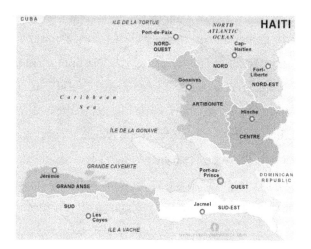

Economy

"Two-thirds of all Haitians depend on the agricultural sector, mainly small-scale subsistence farming, and remain vulnerable to damage from frequent natural disasters, exacerbated by the country's widespread deforestation."[17] Haiti has an alarming unemployment rate estimated at between 40[18] and 70 percent.[19] Haiti's GDP growth averaged 1.2 percent from 1971 to 2013. This growth rate was much lower than the average of Latin American and Caribbean (LAC) countries or other low-income countries.[20]

Haiti is rich in natural resources. As such, it has great potential in the mineral and metal mining industries. "Based on preliminary exploratory activities, Haiti is expected to have substantial deposits, especially in gold, silver, copper, and aluminum bauxite."[21]

The Haitian Diaspora

Haiti experiences high emigration rates, with over one million Haitians now living overseas, mainly in the United States, Dominican Republic, and Canada.[22] Transfers from the Diaspora are a major source of Haiti's income, representing "a large share of GDP, the largest share among LAC countries, and the fourth-highest in the world in terms of export earnings."[23] Remittances from the Haitian Diaspora amounted to $3.8 billion in 2020 or 23 percent of Haiti's gross domestic product.[24] However, Haiti's migrants tend to be educated, causing a significant "brain drain." Consequently, "individuals with advanced education represent only 3 percent of the resident population in Haiti."[25]

Natural Disasters

Natural disasters are one of the main reasons Haiti receives a lot of foreign aid. "Natural disasters have... hampered Haiti's economic performance over the last forty years."[26] Haiti is very susceptible to natural disasters due to a combination of factors, including deforestation and poor infrastructure. Only one percent of Haiti's original forests is left[27] because of "the systematic deforestation to reveal the hideouts of resistance fighters during the American Occupation (1915-34) and Papa Doc's administration (1957-71)," and because most Haitians still use trees to make charcoal for cooking.[28] In 2008 alone, Tropical Storm Fay, Hurricane Gustav, Hurricane Hanna, and Hurricane Ike ravaged the entire country, causing severe flooding, loss of life, and extensive destruction of property. Losses were estimated at 15 percent of GDP. Then on January 12, 2010, the renowned 7.0 magnitude earthquake hit the densely populated capital. "The earthquake...killed 220,000 people, displaced 1.5 million people, and destroyed the equivalent of 120 percent of GDP."[29] On average, Haiti has more natural disasters per km^2 than other Caribbean countries. Though Haiti shares the same island with the Dominican Republic,

> The number of weather-related disasters from 1971 to 2014 has been more than double in Haiti than in the Dominican Republic, mostly because Haiti experienced more than twice as many floods, as a consequence of a storm, and three times the number of drought periods than the Dominican Republic.30

"Overall, based on available historic data, weather-related disasters are estimated to have caused damages and losses amounting to about 2 percent of GDP on average per year during 1975-2012."[31]

Politics

Haiti's political history is a long list of coups, presidential assassinations, dictatorships, and US occupations (1915-34; 1994-5). "Since 1806, fifty-four presidents have been elected. Only nine have completed a full term. The United States had a hand in forcing five presidents out of office."[32]

In the most recent chapter of Haiti's political instability, Haitian president Jovenel Moïse was assassinated in his home on July 7, 2021. Reports are that the assailants were foreign mercenaries.[33] Moïse was installed as Haiti's 58th president in 2017, one year after he had first been elected to office. But those election results were annulled.[34] An interim president had been in place during this period. In January 2021, his opponents insisted that his five-year term had ended, but Moïse maintained that it should end in 2022.[35]

This latest episode in Haiti's political saga is another setback for the country. "Empirical investigations...imply that Haiti would have grown 1.2 percentage points faster if it had achieved an average level of political stability."[36]

In chapter 2, we'll learn more about Haitian culture and worldview and the foundational role these play in the everyday lives of Haitians.

CHAPTER 2: HAITIAN CULTURE

"Pi bonè se granm maten" (Get an early start on the day).

Haitians typically get up well before the crack of dawn to fetch water from the community well and get a head start on the day. People wake up in the dead of night to iron their clothes while there is state electricity. Many food vendors start preparing the day's meal at 3 or 4 a.m. in the morning. If someone stays in bed beyond sunrise, they are considered lazy! In keeping with this "early bird" custom, most churches have their main service at 6 a.m. in the morning.

Haiti is a very close-knit, communal society full of hard-working people. One of the first things a visitor may notice when they meet a Haitian is that Haitians introduce themselves with their family name first, then their first name. Like other communal cultures around the world, notably in Asia and Africa, family and community are more important than individuality. "Konbit," a community workday, is still popular in the countryside, where people come together to work on someone's farm one day and their neighbor's farm the next. As they say in Haiti, *"Vwazinaj se fanmi"*—"Neighbors are family." Another sign of communal culture is that many families prefer to live in close proximity to each other for their entire lives. In Haiti, it is normal that as families grow, siblings build their houses in the same yard or add an extension to the family home and raise their children together.

Because of their communal culture, perfect strangers in Haiti tend to interact in ways reserved for close friends or acquaintances in other cultures. I was getting ready to cross a very busy thoroughfare recently when a lady came up and said, "Kite m' janbe ave w' souple" (Can you help me cross the road, please?). The minute I said "Sure," she took my hand, and we crossed together. "Mesi anpil!" (Thanks a lot!) And she was gone! I see another example of this whenever I travel in Haiti's colorful *tap-taps* (pick-up trucks converted into mini buses for public transport). Instead of letting you travel hunched over in the low, over-crowded *tap-tap*, perfect strangers offer to let you sit on their knees for the duration of the ride.

From an early age, children are taught to look out for their younger siblings or cousins. Every day, older brothers and sisters take their young siblings to and from kindergarten or primary school, carrying them in their arms or on their backs in the sweltering heat and dust. On their way home from school, they buy them little treats and talk about their day at school.

Haitians are ingenious. In the daily thoroughfare, you'll see things like motorcycles stacked high with lumber or men pushing large makeshift wheelbarrows loaded with more than forty mattresses! Beneath the hustle and bustle of daily life as people try to eke out a living is the common worldview or belief system that governs people's lives. Two key aspects of the Haitian worldview are Voodoo and patron-client relationships.

Chicken!

I remember we had a devout Christian woman working for us at home. One day, she went into the backyard and saw a chicken. Guenson proceeded to shoo it in the direction of the gate to let it out. She said, "No! Don't let it get away! You don't know where it came from. Let the dogs go so they can kill it." She thought the chicken was sent mystically into our yard to harm us. But we said, "Even though our concrete wall is high, a chicken could easily fly into the yard from next door." Chickens fly! A hilarious fact, I must admit, I found out only after coming to Haiti! Every evening, free-roaming fowls fly into trees for the night. But our friend was not convinced; she was on high alert for any other mystical sightings or happenings. Haitian Voodoo is deeply embedded in the fabric of Haitian society. Whether people profess to be Christians or not, they usually adhere to some aspect of Voodoo.

One of the most fascinating things I observed when I first moved to Haiti was the proliferation of Voodoo establishments in every community and how openly people practiced magic and sold Voodoo paraphernalia everywhere. I had a similar reaction while visiting New Orleans in 2009, by the way. In Jamaica, we have an equivalent of Voodoo called "Obeah," but it is generally considered taboo and is mostly relegated to the fringes of society—the countryside and Maroon villages. So, hearing people beating Voodoo drums rhythmically and tirelessly all night, almost every night, in the mountains near my home (in the city) was very new to me. There are also many sacred Voodoo sites across Haiti with trees, springs, waterfalls, and caves dedicated to various gods in the Voodoo pantheon.

Worldview

Worldview may be defined as "the fundamental cognitive, affective, and evaluative presuppositions a group of people makes about the nature of things, and which they use to order their lives."[37] People's worldview serves six fundamental purposes in their lives. It provides answers to their ultimate questions; it gives them emotional security; it validates their deepest cultural norms; it helps integrate their culture; it monitors cultural change; and finally, it provides psychological reassurance that the world is truly as they see it, giving a sense of peace. People's worldviews "declare the way things really are and are true in an ultimate sense and are "based on [their] experiences, assumptions, and logics."[38] A child's worldview is already established by age five.

Haitian Voodoo was given the same official status as Catholicism and Protestantism in 1987.[39] This ancient religion is also practiced by some 30 million people in the West African nations of Benin, Togo, Nigeria, and Ghana. In Benin, it is recognized as an official religion. In fact, many of the gods in Haitian Voodoo are directly derived from African religions, for example, *Ogou,* the Nigerian god of war, and *Ezili,* the beautiful water goddess of love from both Benin and Nigeria. When Voodoo was suppressed by the Catholic church in Haiti, the Haitian slaves disguised their worship of African spirits by identifying them with Catholic saints, hence the syncretism or intermingling of Catholicism and Voodoo in Haiti. For example, *Damballah*, Benin's python god becomes Saint Patrick, while *Ezili* becomes the Virgin Mary.[40] Voodoo is also found among the African diaspora in the Americas, such as Cuba (Vodú), Brazil (Vodum), Puerto Rico (Vudú), Louisiana (Voodoo), and, as mentioned before, Jamaica (Obeah). Interestingly, Jamaican and Haitian history are connected by a Jamaican runaway slave, Boukman, who officiated the infamous Voodoo ceremony, which launched Haiti's battle of independence.

Animism

Voodoo is based on animism and magic rituals. "Broadly speaking, magic is the control of this-worldly forces... by the proper use of chants, amulets, and rituals."[41] *Animism* may be defined as "a belief in spirit beings which indwell everything and everyone."[42] While Haitian Voodoo concedes that there is one supreme Being, *Bondye* (literally, Good God), "devotees never attempt to contact him for help" but are rather preoccupied with the myriad of lesser spirits, known as *lwas*, which are perceived to be more in touch with human realities.[43] "Vodou posits a dynamic and organic view of reality, in which all events and conditions, whether natural, spiritual, or social, are believed to be animated by spiritual forces."[44] It teaches that "personal spiritual beings and impersonal forces have power over human affairs and, consequently, that human beings must discover what beings and forces are influencing them in order to determine future action, frequently, to manipulate their power."[45]

Voodoo does not place much emphasis on the afterlife but is rather preoccupied with the urgent everyday needs of its adherents. "Death does not constitute a hope for a future and better life. To live here and now is the most important concern of African religious activities and beliefs...There is neither paradise to be hoped for nor hell to be feared in the hereafter."[46] Unlike Judeo-Christian faiths, in Voodoo, there is no divine judgment awaiting a person after they die; as such, there are no eternal consequences for one's moral choices on earth. There is no divine justice or settling of accounts to hope for after this life. The only justice one can count on is what you can exact for yourself now through magic or other means. Another central belief in Voodoo is reincarnation, where the spirits of ancestors are reborn in their children.[47]

Hiebert (2008) explains that "Our modern temptation is to see magic as meaningless, as childish fantasies and prelogical thought."[48] I concur. Like many foreigners, when I first moved to Haiti, I saw Voodoo as the empty pagan superstitions of backward people. But on closer observation, I realized that magic is their effort to understand and control the chaotic world and circumstances they find themselves in. In Haiti, where life is so unpredictable, with natural disasters, political upheavals, lack of proper medical services, debilitating economic conditions, there is a lot of fear and uncertainty. "Something bad can happen, and it most likely will."

People are vividly aware of the existence of evil forces. Voodoo is their attempt to control their circumstances by appeasing evil spirits in order to live in peace.

In explaining the rise of occultism in America, particularly during the COVID-19 pandemic, Yale psychology professor James Alcock explained that "in times of uncertainty, people have historically looked to the occult to 'get some kind of answer about the future... something that's reassuring in some way.'"[49] Pam Grossman, host of The Witch Wave podcast and author of *Waking the Witch: Reflections on Women, Magic and Power*, makes a similar observation. She states that "Often during times of political turmoil, people turn to witchcraft and alternative spirituality."[50] With Haiti's constant political instability, this explanation may go a long way in explaining Haitians' penchant for Voodoo.

Voodoo and Healing

Voodoo thrives in contexts where medical facilities are inadequate or lacking. For example, Haiti's second largest city, Cap-Haitian, has only one public hospital for a population of close to one million people. There is a proliferation of clinics and private health centers, many with outdated or no medical equipment at all and no state electricity to run them, anyway. In this context rife with medical misdiagnoses and witchcraft discourses, doctors are renowned for telling their patients, "Madam, this sickness is not for a doctor. Don't you have an ancestral village?" In their desperation, people turn to witch doctors for relief. This was the sordid experience of a teenage girl in our church. I will call her Mary.

Mary was born and grew up in the rural part of North Haiti with her mother and father. At nine months old, she started having fainting spells. As she grew up, she had difficulties learning in school. Whenever the time came for her to take her final exams, she had fainting spells in which she lost consciousness for extended periods of time. She repeated several grades several times. They were told that the reason for her suffering was because her grandmother had cast a spell on her. Both her parents worshipped *lwas* (ancestral spirits). When I asked her which *lwas* her parents worshipped, she said they were so many she could not recall all their names.

The situation worsened in 2009 when she became deathly ill. Her father carried her on his back for long distances to consult four *bokos* (witch doctors) at various times during her sickness, paying a lot of money to each. Her father was a poor peasant farmer, but he had to give chickens, goats, or cows for the sacrifices. Nothing worked. The *bokos* gave her many different concoctions to drink from bottles filled with roaches, snakes, and pieces of wood from "the devil's tree" soaked in alcohol. The fourth *boko* made her wear a "vow," which is a special Voodoo garment a worshipper wears for prolonged periods that is supposed to heal or bring good fortune. First, the *boko* sacrificed a goat over her while she had the vow robe on. She wore this robe, which had seven different colors, each representing a spirit, for two months without ever taking it off. Both she and the robe were bloody and filthy. She spent many days in the *boko's* house, sleeping on a thatch mat full of bed bugs that kept biting her but were a part of the sacrifice to be healed. When that did not work, every night at midnight, they took her to the cemetery and laid her on the graves. At this point, both her mother and older sister also became very sick and were also "admitted" with her at the *boko's* house. After a long period of time, Mary's health finally improved. In 2012, her parents decided to give their lives to Christ during a crusade. Since then, Mary has never gotten sick. She herself became a Christian soon after was baptized and has been a fervent Christian since then.

Voodoo beliefs also have a great impact on how many Haitians interpret people's attire and ornamentation. Like many other religions, in Voodoo, one's attire says a lot about one's spirituality. Missionaries and humanitarian workers need to be aware of these cultural cues in order to not send non-verbal messages that may undermine their efforts.

In animistic contexts, witchcraft is not only used to address problems at a personal level but also at the organizational level. We will explore this in the next chapter.

CHAPTER 3: WITCHCRAFT AND FOREIGN AID

"Avan ou ri moun bwete, gade jan ou mache" (Before you laugh at
someone limping, look at how you walk).
—Don't be quick to judge others.

Anthropologist Erica James (2012) conducted very revealing
research into the interaction of witchcraft and humanitarian
aid in Haiti. She explains that "Witchcraft, sorcery, and magic
are foundational anthropological categories describing cultural
practices employed to control flows of power in a society."[51]
Ultimately, witchcraft is preoccupied with how health, wealth,
and justice are distributed in a community. "Witchcraft discourses
incorporate general concerns about uncertainty, scarcity, and risk,
and the ambiguous relationship between hidden and transparent
flows of power."[52]

Witchcraft includes the channeling of occult power to not
only grant clients' fortune but also to determine if their misfortune
is a result of such supernatural activity by someone else. As such,
the prevalence of witchcraft foments rumors, gossip, and scandal
concerning accusations of witchcraft, sorcery, or magic that can lead
to violence.

Contrary to popular perception, witchcraft discourses and
practices are not limited to remote small-scale village societies.
James (2012) cited numerous studies recording an intensification of
witchcraft discourses in postcolonial African states "as well as a rise in
suspicion, paranoia, and conspiracy theories regarding political and

economic practices in postsocialist and Western neoliberal states."[53] In the contemporary context of "millennial capitalism," witchcraft discourses are preoccupied with the unequal distribution of wealth arising from "the workings of insidious forces, of potent magical technologies and mysterious modes of accumulation, of sorcery of one or another sort."[54]

Witchcraft discourses feature prominently not only in political and economic domains but also in the "compassion economy."[55] Here, countries that consider themselves "secure" use military and humanitarian measures to intervene in "insecure" countries in order to mitigate against international risks and to "reengineer post-socialist, post-authoritarian, post-conflict, and post-disaster states."[56] However, these processes are often shrouded by a lack of transparency and, despite brokering deals for vulnerable people and nation-states, the decision-makers are ultimately not accountable to them. After extensive research in Haiti, James' (2012) thesis is that the workings of humanitarian agencies—"well-intentioned activities that nonetheless include opaque bureaucratic practices and competition over knowledge, scarce resources, and institutional territory"— inadvertently propagate negative witchcraft discourses. James (2012) coined the term "bureaucraft" to describe the combination of witchcraft, bureaucracy, and secrecy used by both foreign aid providers and foreign aid recipients in "compassion economies."[57]

In her research, James studied two large medical organizations in Port-au-Prince. She found that misunderstandings about the history and motives of the Human Rights Fund (HRF), a medical NGO funded by USAID, led to "accusations of malfeasance and threats of violence that are components of malevolent "bureaucraft."[58] Eventually, rampant rumors and violent threats in the context of political instability led to the closing of the rehabilitation program of the HRF. A few months later, a movement emerged that opposed the entire HRF organization, accusing the US of "occult" activities, and orchestrating the 1991 coup d'état; and the lead doctors of swapping out medications with ones that would kill the victims (James, 2012). Eventually, the organization had to close its operations.

James (2012) concludes that because of inadequate transparency and compassion in contexts of scarcity and instability,

> Humanitarian and development interventions can foment, rather than quell social insecurity...A central paradox of humanitarian aid [is that] through its discourse and practices the aid apparatus can exacerbate cycles of economic decline and political and criminal instability, thereby reproducing the very conditions for military and humanitarian interventions that brought the aid apparatus into being in the first place.[59]

From my personal experience, in 2018, I formed a youth organization to do community clean-ups. For one project, our group comprised of about twenty Haitians and two Caucasians from Youth with a Mission (YWAM). We went to clean-up the Vertieres Park, a very significant historical location that was the site of the Haitian battle of Independence. When we got there, however, we encountered strong verbal opposition. Several people argued that it was shameful for us to have "blans" (Caucasians) coming to do clean-up and that the "blans" were the ones who brought us along as puppets for a fundraising or publicity campaign. One man hurled insults in a loud voice for the entire two hours that we were there. The local representative threatened us and later lodged a complaint to his supervisor that we brought a group of "blans" to this important historical site without his permission. His biggest concern was that we took away bags of garbage which was suspicious because he claimed that some White people had taken dirt from the site before to perform occult ceremonies overseas in order to dominate Haiti.

Judge Not

Westerners tend to frown upon Voodoo—ominously labeled "Black" magic—while they accept other supposedly benign forms of magic and the occult—"White" magic, as it is called. Many North Americans, professing Christians or not, religiously read their daily horoscope with their morning coffee. Others think nothing of getting a palm reading. All these are forms of divination—using spiritual forces to foretell the future—which abound in Western industrialized countries. Horoscopes, palm reading, Ouija boards, tarot cards, occult movies, and books are a multi-billion-dollar business in Europe and North America. An article charmingly entitled "The occult is having a moment" reveals that the "psychic services" industry is currently worth $2.2 billion in the US alone. It grew about one-half a percent every year since 2016 and is expected to more than double that rate, with 2.6 percent growth in 2021.[60] For example, Cardenas, a witch from Southern California, charges $85 for a forty-minute tarot reading, $55 for a spell consultation, and anywhere from $155 to $321 for a spell. He describes his prices as "cheap" compared to other places.[61]

> The occult has become more popular, especially on social media, and with apps like Co-Star...What was once a crime punished by execution is now a well-established part of mainstream US culture. Witches have gained massive followings—the HoodWitch has over 455,000 followers on Instagram alone—and in some places "What's your astrology sign?" is as common a question as "What do you do for a living?" The occult isn't something scary or fringe anymore, it's part of our children's entertainment in books like "Harry Potter" and movies like "Halloweentown."[62]

In South America, Santeria worshippers participate in animal sacrifices similar to Voodoo for protection or to cause others harm. In Asia, Buddhist priests have a special dance to ward off evil spirits. In Turkey, stores sell blue amulets for people to hang in their homes to ward off the "evil eye," which people in Haiti call *malveyan*. For example, The Duchess of Sussex, Meghan Markle, was spotted wearing a $1500 gold-and-diamond Eye of Protection bracelet and, on another occasion, a Didem Evil Eye bracelet. According to the bracelet's description, "Legend has it that the evil eye works as a shield for envy, reflecting any evil back to where it came from and protecting its owner from any harmful spirits."[63] Others see nothing wrong with wearing lucky charms, such as Feng Shui bracelets and rings, to procure success or deter misfortune. All these are magic in one form or another.

Jesus told his disciples, "Judge not" (Matthew 7:1, ESV), meaning, "Do not write others off for their sins." It does not mean that others are justified in doing wrong, and we should leave them alone. It means we should be aware of our own wrongdoings and hold ourselves to the same standards we hold others to. "For in the same way you judge others, you will be judged, and with the measure you use, it will be measured to you" (Matthew 7:2).

In the next chapter, we will explore the second dominant aspect of the Haitian worldview, a patron-client social contract.

CHAPTER 4: PATRON-CLIENT CULTURE

"Yon men lave lòt" (One hand washes the other)
—We need each other.

Renowned Christian anthropologist Paul Hiebert explains that patron-client relationships usually exist in agrarian settings where the "patrons are landowners who organize the farming" and are "responsible for the survival and well-being of [their] workers."[64] The clients, on the other hand, are expected to not only work in the fields and at home but to render all sorts of miscellaneous services to the patron, including "fight[ing] for him if his rivalries erupt into open violence."[65] There are many similarities between this description and life in Haiti where people literally call their rich benefactors "patron." In agrarian societies like Haiti, where two-thirds of the population depends on the agricultural sector, patron-client relationships thrive.

Hossain (2004) explains the intricate relationships and balance of power in patron-client societies:

> In a society where most are very poor, the very rich can—and are [in Bangladesh] expected to—treat poorer people as clients...To be a client is to defer and obey as a means of attracting protection against crisis, or for help with investment in the future. To be a patron is to have control over clients' labour, lives and leisure.[66]

There are four distinguishing features of the patron-client relationship. First, the personal and moral value of the relationship is greater than the favors exchanged. Second, there are the roles of deference and authority. Third, the favors exchanged are different but mutually beneficial. Finally, the patron's favorable perception of the relationship determines how it is portrayed publicly.[67] The patron-client culture is why successful family members who have migrated to urban centers or overseas are expected to support their poor relatives back home or in the countryside.

Despite being predominant in agrarian settings, the patron-client culture, like animism, is able to integrate and adapt in contemporary societies. In the cosmopolitan context, where aspiring leaders or patrons may not be able to provide their clients with land to work, they leverage their influence in the private or public sector to offer jobs or other favors.[68] This bartering of favors, when institutionalized, has been shown to have a detrimental effect on state and market efficiency. The patron-client view of relationships is often the basis of cronyism and misusing institutional resources for personal favors.

According to Hossain (2004), resident foreign aid donors, by virtue of their high social status and economic means, are drawn into patron-client societies as patrons. As such, they are often approached by locals for different forms of patronage, including cash, jobs, and foreign travel. Some foreign aid donors are ambivalent, while others are uncomfortable about the constant demands made on them by locals, feeling that they are singled out because of their "whiteness."

However, these "responsibilities of the rich are standard in all unequal relationships" in patron-client societies.[69]

Finally, many foreign aid donors observe that foreign aid recipients "frequently agree to donor conditions which they later fail to meet, or which they have never had any intention of meeting."[70] This can be a form of deference required in patron-client cultures or a form of passive resistance.

In chapter 5, we will begin to explore foreign aid recipient perceptions in Haiti with a trip back into the country's colonial past.

CHAPTER 5: HAITI'S COLONIAL PAST

"Lafimen pa janm leve san dife" (Where there's smoke, there's fire).
—There's a reason for everything.

It is impossible to understand Haiti's current condition without pulling back the curtains on its history. Haiti's colonial past is the backdrop to how many Haitians perceive foreign aid and foreign aid donors. I often wondered why Haiti, as the first slave colony to win its independence, was still "stuck in the past." After all, other small islands like Jamaica, Barbados, and Trinidad and Tobago got their independence less than sixty years ago during my father's lifetime, while Haiti has been independent for nearly 220 years. But then I realized that being handed your independence and fighting for it "tooth and nail" are two different things. Plus, Haiti's history of slavery and foreign domination is a revolving door that was never fully shut. Long after the trauma of Spanish and French enslavement, the festering wounds of colonial abuse have never fully healed because they have continually been reopened over the past 200 years.

"Pearl of the Antilles"

At the height of its economic expansion in the 1700s, Haiti was called "The Pearl of the Antilles" for its unmatched wealth and beauty among the other Caribbean islands.[71]

So significant was the agricultural yield of the colony that, by the latter half of the eighteenth century, it was exporting 163 million pounds of sugar annually, a figure representing nearly 60 percent of the world's sugar consumption…It also produced three times more indigo than the two Carolinas combined, and coffee and cotton crops that equaled in value the annual tobacco crops of both Maryland and Virginia…by 1789, its 8000 plantations were producing more than 40 percent of France's foreign trade.[72]

This production was, of course, fueled by African slaves, with Haiti some years receiving up to half of the slaves from the Trans-Atlantic slave trade.[73] There were ten times as many slaves and *affrachis*, or mulattoes, than whites.[74] The majority of slaves in Haiti were born in Africa because the inhumane conditions on the plantations prevented natural population growth.[75]

Slavery and Battle of Independence

French enslavement was notorious for its brutality, outdoing even the Spanish.[76] A visitor to the island around 1790 described waking up to an "infernal melody:"

The crowing of the rooster: the cracking of the whip, the choking of screams, the deafening groans of the Negroes who experience the beginning of the day only to curse it, who are reminded of their feeling for existence only by painful sensations...[77]

A former slave from that era described vividly.

> Have they not hung up men with heads downward, drowned them in sacks, crucified them on planks, buried them alive, crushed them in mortars? Have they not forced them to eat [feces]? And, having flayed them with the lash, have they not cast them alive to be devoured by worms, or onto anthills, or lashed them to stakes in the swamp to be devoured by mosquitos? Have they not thrown them into boiling cauldrons of cane syrup? Have they not put men and women inside barrels studded with spikes and rolled them down mountainsides into the abyss? Have they not consigned these miserable blacks to man-eating dogs until the latter, sated by human flesh, left the mangled victims to be finished off with bayonet and poniard?[78]

This brutality intensified after the French Revolution of 1789, with its motto of "liberty, equality, and fraternity for all," emboldened some slaves to revolt against the cruel conditions on the plantations.[79]

> Many slaves, judged to be disrespectful to their masters, were forced to eat their own excrement or to drink the saliva of other slaves; others, their bodies covered with

molasses, were tied to active beehives…blazing irons and hot beeswax applied to the heads, arms and shoulders of slaves were common punishments; pregnant women were convicted to such hard labor that often miscarriages resulted.[80]

The horrors of such vicious treatment no doubt leave an indelible mark on the psyche of a people. In their landmark study, a research team at New York's Mount Sinai hospital led by Dr. Rachel Yehuda found that severe trauma, such as in the case of Jews who survived the Holocaust, can alter one's DNA and then be passed on genetically to subsequent generations. Yehuda's work "is the clearest example in humans of the transmission of trauma to a child via what is called 'epigenetic inheritance.'"[81] The lasting impact of French enslavement on the Haitian psyche is demonstrated by the fact that the closest concept of hell in Haitian Voodoo is to be brought back from the dead and be enslaved brutally on a plantation forever. That is, to be turned into a "zombie."

The treatment on the Haitian plantations made both mulattoes as well as slaves increasingly disgruntled with their social conditions. Things came to a head in 1791 when a runaway slave and Voodoo priest from Jamaica, Dutty Boukman, started a rebellion.[82] After the infamous Voodoo ceremony in which a pig was sacrificed and its blood imbibed, the slaves went into the towns and "indiscriminately slaughtered every white man, woman, and child."[83]

The Price of Freedom

In 1804, "after almost thirteen years of war which involved Britain, France, Spain, and the United States and a bitter struggle between the former slaves and their former masters,"[84] Haiti won its independence and its place in history as the world's first free Black Republic. France, however, refusing to accept their defeat, sent a heavily armed military detachment to demand that Haiti pay an "indemnity" of 150 million gold francs or suffer a crippling embargo imposed by France, Britain, and the United States.[85] This sum was ten times what the United States had paid for Louisiana, more than eight times France's annual budget, and more than ten times Haiti's annual budget.[86] "Over the next 120 years, as much as 80 percent of Haiti's revenues went to paying off this debt."[87] The fledgling nation took out high-interest loans from French banks to pay this debt which was not fully paid until 1947. Though the payment was later reduced to ninety million gold francs, contemporary assessments have revealed that after interest payments, Haiti ended up paying more than twice that amount.[88]

Considered "the greatest heist in history,"[89] these steep payments have "caused irreversible damage to the country's economy... To this day, Haiti's economy has not fully recovered from these damages."[90] Despite this "freedom tax," France did not recognize Haiti's sovereignty until 1825; and Haiti did not receive US diplomatic recognition until 1862.[91] Numerous calls have been made for France to make reparations for this sum which is equivalent to $21 billion today.[92] But these appeals have fallen on deaf ears.

New Oppressors

Jean-Jacques Dessalines, a former slave who was one of the country's foremost revolutionaries, became its first (self-proclaimed) emperor from 1804 to 1807. However, he was assassinated two years later, and the country was divided by two rival leaders—Henri Christophe and Alexandre Pétion. During this post-independence period, Haiti had so much political and economic clout that it was able to take control of the entire island of Hispaniola, making the Dominican Republic its subject from 1822 to 1844. This fact still remains a root of bitterness between the neighboring countries to this day.

After the French were ousted, the mulatto class stepped into the power vacuum militarizing agriculture and creating a peasant economy. "Peasantry" connotes,

> The cultivation of the land by uneducated persons whose families have occupied a low status in a highly structured society in which it is difficult for them to climb the social ladder...a people is described as a peasant society when at least half its population fulfills these criteria.[93]

A new form of slavery emerged, with the peasants working under grueling conditions to meet production quotas established by mulatto bureaucrats and landowners. Burney (2012), building on the works of postcolonial thinkers such as Said and Fanon, described the persona of "the nationalist bourgeoisie, who often ran the new countries with a callous, exploitative tyranny reminiscent of the departed masters. This native elite had replaced colonial rulers with an exploitative neocolonialism based on class differences and social standing."[94] Postcolonial scholars observed that "It is the lack of social conscience that often enables the native elite to become the new oppressors, dictators, and power brokers in newly independent societies."[95]

The rigid social structure that resulted in post-independence is still largely in place today and is the main reason for Haiti's constant class struggles and political upheavals.[96] The same rhetoric of freedom from slavery and the same methods of burning down property during protests are still widely employed today.

The American Occupations

Haiti was the military protectorate of the United States from 1915 to 1934 and again from 1994 to 1995.

According to US Department of State Archives (2001-2009), "The United States Government had been interested in Haiti for decades prior to its occupation... to secure a US defensive and economic stake in the West Indies."[97] The American government grew increasingly concerned about the possibility of "foreign rule of Haiti" due to Haiti's "close connection to France" and "increased German activity and influence" in the country.[98]

After a period of increased political instability, the United States' president, Woodrow Wilson, ordered US military control of Haiti.

According to US Department of State Archives, on December 17, 1914, officials of the National City Bank of New York...accompanied by US Marines, arrived in Haiti on board the navy destroyer *Machias*...They entered the Banque Nationale in Port-au-Prince"[99] and "removed $500,000 ... for safe-keeping in New York, thus giving the US control of the bank."[100] There is no mention of if or when this money was returned. The US Department of State Archives further reveal that in 1915,

> President Wilson sent the US Marines to Haiti, claiming the invasion was an attempt to prevent anarchy. In reality the Wilson administration was protecting US assets in the area and preventing a possible German invasion.[101]

American government interference in Haitian socio-political affairs and the nefarious consequences are a well-recorded fact in the annals of history.

> Since the turn of the twentieth century many US decisions concerning Haiti have helped initiate political instability and violence. One example of the lasting legacy of the American occupation of Haiti-from 1915 to 1934—was the reestablishment of its military...which inflicted considerable damage on the country and deposed a number of presidents, including Elie Lescot in 1946, Dumarsais Estime in 1950, and Jean Bertrand Aristide in 1991.[102]

While the nineteen-year occupation brought some good results, these were outweighed by a host of negatives, including putting in a "puppet president" as the head of state and responding viciously by killing thousands of protestors who opposed the occupation.[103] In addition, racist "Jim-Crow laws that continued to oppress blacks in the American South were applied to all nonwhites in Haiti."[104]

The atrocities committed by American troops during the US occupations continue to engender many Haitians' resentment towards the United States and foreign governments in general. Chief among these infractions was forcing "peasants to labor on road-building projects,"[105] for which Haitians coined the term "*korve*" which refers to all types of demeaning work. Americans were also responsible for killing all the native black pigs based on claims that they had African swine fever.[106] These pigs were the source of many Haitians' livelihood. The Haitian version of events is that the Americans killed the pigs in order to make the country dependent on food imports from that country.

Unlike Bangladesh,[107] (American) foreign aid donors have had a very close relationship with the local elites (Haitian mulattos), whom they considered "more civilized" than the Black masses.[108] The Marine occupation legitimized the mulatto elite's control of the government, setting in place a repressive ethnic and economic system that persists today.[109] The 1915 American occupation of Haiti, which was "self-interested, oppressive, sometimes brutal, caused problems that lasted past its lifetime, and never paid any reparations for its crimes."[110]

The Americans left in 1934 but remained in control of Haiti's national finances until 1947[111]—coincidentally, the same year Haiti finished making "indemnity" payments to France.[112] Leaving no system in place for political transition or national leadership, the situation in Haiti grew increasingly turbulent following the departure of the Americans. After a six-month period between 1956 and 1957 in which five governments took power, the United States helped install François "Papa Doc" Duvalier as president.[113] François Duvalier and his son Jean-Claude ("Baby Doc") had a combined thirty-year dictatorial reign characterized by thousands of political assassinations, "massive corruption, cronyism, and repression of human rights."[114] "Yet the United States continued to provide the country with aid in order to maintain it as an ally in the fight against communism."[115] Foreign aid amounted to 70 percent of the Haitian national treasury in 1970 and increased to $35.5 million by 1975.[116] However, because of rampant corruption, little of this aid reached the impoverished populace.

The Duvalier Legacy

One of the most insidious legacies of the Duvalier era is institutionalized inequality. Under the Duvalier regime, business contracts in key industries were doled out as bargaining chips to Haitian elites and foreigners alike.[117] "Many of the same elite families who dominated the Haitian economy during the era of Duvalier in the 1970s remain in control of large segments of the economy today."[118]

The roots of Haiti's poverty run deep, to its colonial history, its 200-year dependence on the major Western industrial powers and its narrowly-based oligarchy. In the latter half of the twentieth century, the oligarchy has maintained tight control of the economy with the sometimes implicit, sometimes explicit- but always crucial-support of the United States.[119]

This small group of Haitian elites also maintain their dominance through monetary aid from the United States.[120]

As a result, Haiti is one of the most polarized countries in the world.[121] The country's Gini index, which measures "the extent to which the distribution of income (or, in some cases, consumption expenditure) among individuals or households within an economy deviates from a perfectly equal distribution,"[122] is 0.65.[123] While Haiti is the poorest country in the western hemisphere, it also has more millionaires per capita than many other developing countries.[124] "One percent of Haiti's population controls almost half of the country's wealth."[125] The elites are the Haitian bourgeois class, who are mostly descendants of French colonialists and businesspeople of foreign descent. These people, about 200 families (10,000 individuals), control the private sector. They operate roughly 500 businesses that account for 90 percent of the country's imports.[126] Most of the upper class receives religious legitimacy from the Catholic Church and economic legitimacy from politicians.[127]

High levels of inequality have grave consequences for a country's well-being. "An overriding channel through which such a high inequality level has apparently affected growth negatively in the Republic of Haiti is via the social tensions it breeds and the ensuing political instability, which do not create an atmosphere for investment"[128] and therefore impedes growth. Haiti "has evidenced how distributional conflict fostered all sort of instability going from riots, macroeconomic instability, violent airing of grievances, to bloody *coups-d'états*."[129]

French colonialism and the US occupation weakened Haiti's economy and deprived it of control over its industry, trade, and natural resources. The roots of Haiti's "'prickly nationalism,' distrust of foreigners, and an economy largely dependent on foreign assistance" lie in over a century of having its national agenda dictated by outsiders.[130]

Slavery and colonization were two of the main forces which shaped how Haitians perceive foreign involvement in Haiti. In the next chapter, we will examine the lens through which many foreigners view Haiti—Western mass media.

CHAPTER 6: WESTERN MEDIA AND FOREIGN AID

"Lè mayigwen mòde ou sou nen, ou pa ka ba l' kou fò" (If a mosquito is biting your nose, you can't hit it hard).
—Solve a problem without making matters worse.

Haiti Stigmatized by Western Media

Haiti's biggest problem is not poverty, crime, or political instability—it's a bad reputation. Haiti is falsely portrayed by Western media as the most crime-ridden, disease-infested country in the region.

Media can be used as a powerful tool of cultural imperialism, which, in turn, has direct bearing on how foreign aid donors treat beneficiaries, how beneficiaries perceive themselves as aid recipients, and the recipient country's ability to develop economically.[131] "Visual culture can be employed as a means of disciplinary power," and photography has been used by former colonial powers as means of controlling space and maintaining "social hegemony."[132] "A particular set of countries have had the power, means, and opportunity to construct and disseminate representations of Haiti" as fundamentally defective and inherently dependent on foreign aid.[133] Understanding media portrayal of Haiti is crucial because the perceptions of others greatly impact self-perceptions. Numerous experiments in social psychology have demonstrated that "When we expect to be viewed as inferior, our abilities seem to be diminished."[134]

Potter (2009), in her study entitled *Voodoo, Zombies, and Mermaids: US Newspaper Coverage of Haiti* conducted a critical geopolitical analysis of how Haiti is portrayed in US newspapers. "Critical studies have shown that representation in the media can greatly impact the conventional wisdom surrounding a place and legitimize social inequalities."[135]

Western Media and Haiti's Economic Decline

Media is an important means by which the American public learns about other parts of the world and hence shapes public perceptions and informs political decisions. Importantly, how a country is portrayed by the media "affects the US general public's attitude toward matters like tourism, migration, investments, and the establishment of businesses."[136] Despite the gravity of its impact, "In addition to reinforcing ideological convictions or views, the media also tend to report solely for entertainment value."[137]

One case in point is the false media reports "about Haiti being the point of origin of the North American HIV-AIDS epidemic," which stigmatized the country and devastated its tourism industry in the 1980s.[138] From the 1950s to 1983, Haiti was "a prime Caribbean tourist destination," with tourism being the country's second-largest source of foreign revenue.[139] The US Centers for Disease Control (CDC) published an "inflammatory assessment of Haitians as a member of the 'four Hs,' who were high risks for HIV infection (homosexuals, heroin users, hemophiliacs, and Haitian)."[140] By the time these erroneous conceptions were corrected, they had received much less publicity than the false reports, and the damage was already done. Haiti's tourism has never fully recovered.

Potter (2009) found that most newspapers depicted Haiti as a "failed state" unable to govern itself. The most common words the US newspapers used to describe Haiti were *violence*, or some form of the word *poor* or *blood*.[141] Yet the press largely ignored the historical context of Haiti being a pawn in the geopolitical programs of the United States, Canada, and France.

More devastating is the impact media has on how Haitians perceive themselves. Most of the newspaper articles Potter examined used Haiti's demise to portray Haitians as "somehow 'other' than the rest of humanity.[142]"

> One Haitian American writer, Edwidge Danticat, de-scribed the shame she feels when revealing her native identity. "It was very hard... 'Haitian' was like a curse. People were calling you 'Frenchy, go back to the banana boat,' and a lot of kids would lie about where they came from. They would say anything but Haitian."[143]

Media Coverage Of The 2010 Earthquake

Anthropologist and Haiti expert, Dr. Timothy Schwartz (2017), drew similar conclusions as Potter when he described the interna-tional media coverage after the 2010 earthquake in Haiti:

> The mainstream media did what it always does to Haiti: in the name of selling newspapers and increasing television viewership it re-affirmed the image of Haiti that it created, an image of the macabre, the mad, and the malevolent; indeed, the "island of the damned" where in the best of times "murder, rape and voodoo" prevailed.[144]

Schwartz further revealed that the death rate from the 2010 earthquake was grossly exaggerated by the Haitian government, Western media, and international NGOs for sensational effect and profit-making motives. Major news channels and large NGOs claimed the death rate was between 200,000 and 316,000 people. But in late 2010, Dr. Schwartz and a specially commissioned survey team estimated, with a 99 percent probability, that the earthquake death toll was between 46,190 and 84,961. In his book, *The Great Haiti Humanitarian Aid Swindle*, Dr. Schwartz explains that the inflated death toll suggests "falsified data at the highest levels of the government and cover-ups at the highest level of the press."[145]

Media Portrayal of Disease in Haiti

One recent case in point about the bias of Western media against Haiti is the coverage of the COVID-19 global pandemic. As COVID-19 reached Haiti's shores, Western media outlets and international NGOs seemed as excited as dog hounds at the scent of blood. In May 2020, when Haiti had only one hundred confirmed cases and eleven deaths, CNN published a gripping article of doom and gloom about the "perfect storm approaching" Haiti.[146] Experts predicted an impending "peak" with over 20,000 deaths.[147] They started digging graves in Port-au-Prince to prepare. But thank God for empty graves. In June, when the predictions of organizations such as the World Health Organization and Doctors Without Borders fell through, the media scrambled to explain the death toll of "only fifty-four" as "not reflect[ing] the reality on the ground."[148] At the same time, the Dominican Republic, next door with similar population size, had *ten times* Haiti's death rate yet received none of this negative press.

"Almost 160,000 people entered Haiti from the Dominican Republic between March 17 and May 31 [2020]"[149] when the Dominican Republic closed down, and many Haitians were deported or fled the outbreak there. "During that same period, Haitians crossed into the Dominican Republic at least 100,000 times, with thousands more likely crossing unofficially."[150] And twice every week, when the borders are open for commerce, thousands of Haitians enter the Dominican Republic to buy and sell merchandise and return home. Additionally, during the pandemic, the Trump administration deported scores of infected Haitians.[151] Yet somehow, the virus has not spread in Haiti as it has elsewhere. Underreporting or undertesting cannot explain this because if the virus had spread in congested Port-au-Prince anywhere near what it did in other places, like New York or India, there would be no way to hide the bodies. They would have piled up in hospitals and funeral homes as they did in those places. Instead, many emergency treatment centers set up in Port-au-Prince by medical NGOs had to be shuttered due to a lack of patients.[152]

"We don't have a large quantity of people who are in bad shape," said Dr. Sophia Cherestal Wooley, deputy medical coordinator for Doctors Without Borders/Médecins Sans Frontières in Port-au-Prince. "They get sick, but they don't get really sick or they are just asymptomatic entirely," said Dr. Mary A. Clisbee, the director of research for Partners in Health, which runs the University Hospital of Mirebalais.[153] Experts are still puzzled about why. Haiti is possibly the only country in the region where the customary greeting is a kiss on the cheek—a kiss of death during a pandemic. So, if there was one country that should have been totally ravaged by COVID-19, it should have been Haiti. Yet,

> A year later (April 2021), despite no vaccines or social distancing, Haiti has one of the lowest death rates from COVID-19 in the world...Only 254 deaths were attributed to COVID-19 in Haiti...a death rate of just 22 per million. In the US the COVID-19 death rate is 1,800 per million, and in parts of Europe, the fatality rate is approaching 3,000 deaths per million.[154]

See Appendix 1 and Figure 2 for a comparison of COVID death rates in the Caribbean.

Figure 2: COVID death rate in selected Caribbean countries[1]

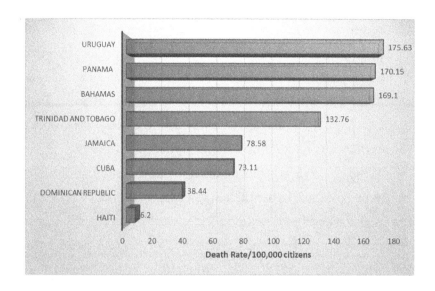

Despite Haiti's low COVID-19 death rate, the CDC gave the country a Level 4 rating (the highest level), stating: "Avoid travel to Haiti...Because of the current situation in Haiti even fully vaccinated travelers may be at risk for getting and spreading COVID-19 variants."[155]

Media Portrayal of Violence in Haiti

Haiti is not only misrepresented by the US media but also by US state agencies. The US Overseas Security Advisory Council reported that Haiti had 757 reported homicides in 2018, a decrease from 2017...

---

[1] As of November 15, 2021

"with 73 percent occurring in the West Department, which includes Port-au-Prince."[156] Based on the population in 2018,[157] this results in a homicide rate of approximately 6.8/100,000 people. In 2019, the United Nations Integrated Office in Haiti (BINUH) reported that "Haiti continues to face high and rising levels of violence" with a total of 910 reported homicides, "a ratio of 9.34 per 100,000 citizens... Two-thirds of those homicides were recorded in the West Department, where criminality is traditionally more prevalent."[158]

OSAC (2019) insists that underreporting is a serious problem in Haiti; therefore, not to use these statistics as a point of comparison. But even if Haiti's reported homicides were tripled, it would still be much less than the homicide rate in US cities such as St. Louis (64.54), Baltimore (58.27), and Birmingham (50.62)[159] (see Figure 3). In other words, if these cities had the same population size as Haiti, they would have many more murders than Haiti. Not to mention the 336 mass shootings (with four or more victims) in the US so far in 2021. This is "roughly two [mass shootings] every day this year"[160]—with more than 230 people fatally shot during the 4th of July holiday weekend alone.[161]

Furthermore, while US cities like New York saw gun violence double in 2020 and had to declare a gun violence state of emergency in July 2021,[162] their reputation does not paint the entire United States or even their entire city as dangerous and overrun with criminals. Whereas violence and political unrest centered almost exclusively in Port-au-Prince, a city of fewer than two million people, is used to stigmatize an entire nation of 11.5 million.

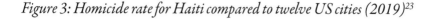

Figure 3: Homicide rate for Haiti compared to twelve US cities (2019)²³

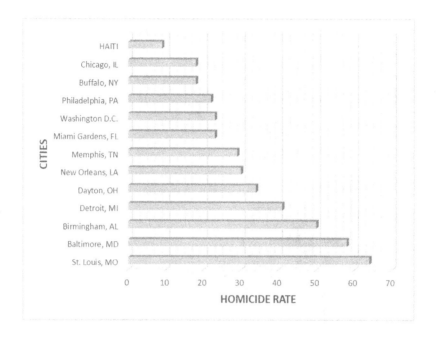

Haiti's homicide rate (6.8 per 100,000 inhabitants in 2018) is also less than Caribbean countries like neighboring Dominican Republic (12.5), Jamaica (47.4), and Venezuela (60.3).[163] In simpler terms, the Dominican Republic, with a slightly smaller population than Haiti, had 1,068 murders in 2018,[164] while Haiti had 743.[165] "In 2019, Jamaica, Trinidad and Tobago, Puerto Rico, and the Dominican Republic registered some of the highest homicide rates in the whole Latin American and Caribbean region."[166] Yet Haiti remains

---

³ These rates were calculated using the FBI's 2019 Crime in the United States data, as well as data from city police officials and the US Census Bureau.

stigmatized as the most crime-ridden country in the region. See Figure 4 for 2020 homicide rates for selected Latin American and Caribbean countries.

Figure 4: Homicide Rate for 12 Latin American and Caribbean countries (2020)[167]

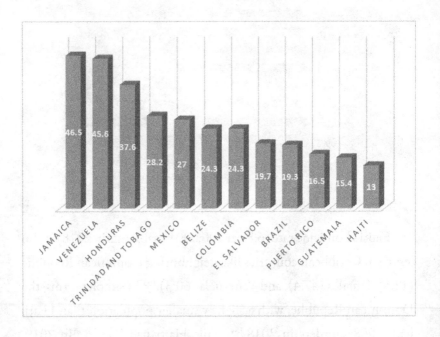

Media Portrayal of Kidnappings in Haiti

Haiti is also labeled as one of the most unsafe countries when it comes to kidnappings. In June 2021, the US Travel Advisory gave the country a Level 4 rating, urging, "Do not travel to Haiti due to kidnapping... Kidnapping is widespread..."[168] But the fact is that kidnappings mainly take place in Port-au-Prince. The "UN Integrated Office in Haiti recorded 234 reported kidnappings in 2020"[169]—a rate of 2.03 per 100,000 citizens. This somehow seems more alarming than the fact that "the United States is ranked as one of the worst countries globally for human trafficking."[170]

> A common misconception about human trafficking is that it does not happen in the United States. This is false, as...it is estimated that 199,000 incidents occur within the United States every year.[171]

Human trafficking is the worst form of kidnapping because victims are kidnapped for sexual exploitation or forced labor.[172] Many are never heard from again. According to statistics from the National Human Trafficking Hotline, in 2019, Nevada had the highest rate of human trafficking (7.50), followed by other states such as Mississippi (4.99), Florida (4.08), Georgia (3.85), and California (3.80).[173] See Figure 5 for the ten US states with the highest human trafficking rates.

Many other developed countries also grapple with high and increasing rates of kidnapping. In 2020, England and Wales had a 7.8 percent increase in kidnappings compared to the previous year. In total, 5,325 adults were kidnapped, and 991 children were abducted, resulting in a kidnapping rate of 8.89—more than three times what it was in 2010[174] and four times the rate in Haiti in 2020.

Figure 5: Human Trafficking rates in US cities compared to the kidnapping rate in Haiti

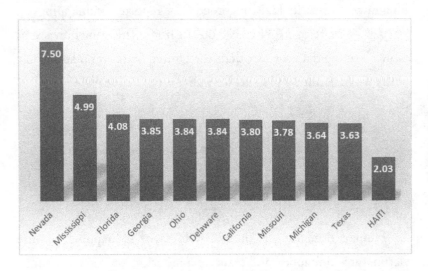

Haitian kidnappings are portrayed more gruesomely than kidnappings elsewhere. For example, Reuters reported a ghastly tale of mass kidnappings in Mexico since the start of 2021. Yet the headline demurely read, "Nearly 3,300 migrants stranded in Mexico were kidnapped, raped or assaulted—report."[175] But after ten clergy were kidnapped in Haiti, then all later released in early 2021, the same newspaper announced: "'Descent into hell:' Kidnapping explosion terrorizes Haiti."[176]

When a country has a large middle class, is clean and modernized, we automatically have a positive perception of its people. When a country is poor, polluted, plus the people speak a completely different language, it is easy to imagine the worst. Appearances drive perception.

Media Portrayal of Political Instability in Haiti

Haiti's political upheavals feature prominently in Western media. "The media describe[s] Haiti as a politically unstable place, full of violence, turmoil, chaos, corruption, and a multitude of other problems."[177]

Haiti's political instability is used by many to justify the labels of Haiti being violent and chaotic when in fact, history has proven that regardless of country or race, rampant injustice and inequality produces "simmering resentment against the [exploitative] class creat[ing] conditions that [are] ripe for revolt."[178] When people feel that their political system is broken and that the justice system is unjust, those frustrations often boil over in counterproductive ways, as the 2021 US Capitol riots demonstrated.

US media reports greatly impact US foreign policy in Haiti. They have been used to inform and justify US intervention throughout the course of Haiti's history.

> Haiti's geographical frame, which establishes the country as the political, economic, and environmental wreck of the western hemisphere, set out to justify US policy toward Haiti. The media's portrayal of Haiti as a political mess and a country in deep poverty work alongside one another. The country's political failures and the violence that often occurs because of that disunion allow the US government to disregard and remove Haitian leaders that fall out of favor.[179]

"An Exceptional Haiti"

According to historian Garland, the portrayals of "an Exceptional Haiti—the poorest, most corrupt, untenable... a 'phantasmagoria of civilization' ... the national manifestation of the frightening, exceptional 'Other'" began after the nation's inception in 1804.[180] One can only surmise that this insidious propaganda about Haiti by Western mass media is part of "a racist conspiracy to put [Haiti] back in [its] place"[181] after being presumptuous enough to demand its independence while Blacks in the rest of the world were docile slaves. Indeed, these representations are a way to obscure the fact that Haiti's condition is "the product of its history: of the nation's founding by enslaved people who overthrew their masters and freed themselves; of the hostility that this revolution generated among the colonial powers surrounding the country."[182] "Haiti's independence was viewed as a threat by all slave-owning countries—the United States included—and its very existence rankled racist sensibilities globally."[183] Haiti became "the black sheep" of the entire Black race.

Media Madness

As the poorest country in the western hemisphere, Haiti has no major international ports or conglomerates, nor is it a regional business hub. What it does have are countless international NGOs eager to prove their legitimacy. Why does Western media have such a keen interest in bad news from Haiti? Somehow Haitian politics and events (only *negative* events, mind you) remain front and center of international news. Who cares? Someone obviously does! There are powerful interest groups—international humanitarian organizations, meddling foreign governments, corrupt Haitian politicians, and greedy local oligopolies—that benefit from Haiti's status as a failed welfare state.

Historically, the US seems to use bad press about Haiti as a tactic to detract attention from how bad things are at home. That was the case for the HIV/AIDS epidemic. And whenever there is an increase in violent crime in the US, journalists seem to turn the spotlight on Haiti to somehow assure the populace that things could be worse. Somehow, when impoverished, illiterate black men kidnap ten people for ransom, it seems more depraved and shocking than when one rich, educated, angry white man opens fire at random, brutally and senselessly killing ten people.

Another illusion commonly used in journalism is the use of the word "abduction" versus "kidnapping." In legal terms,

> When a person is kidnapped, he or she has been <u>taken</u> against his or her will usually through <u>forcible</u> means, by threats against him or her or in some way of deceit... However, a crime of abduction is considered to be when a person has been taken away from his or her original location by persuading him or her, by some act of fraud or with a <u>forceful</u> way that may include violence.[184]

Tomato, *tomato*? Both crimes are the split image of each other, with the only supposed difference being that "While kidnapping often has a ransom for some gain, abduction does not in most cases. Some states do classify ransom demands to be part of abduction cases."[185] "Abduction" is the word of choice when describing the act of taking someone against their will in the US, while "kidnapping" is invariably used when describing the same crime in Haiti and developing countries. "Kidnapping" sounds the fire alarm, while "abduction" sounds benign. No need to alarm the public, right? Regardless of the outcome, the word "kidnapping" portrays a more gruesome crime than an "abduction," even if the kidnapped victim is later released for ransom and the abducted victim is never heard from again. Apparently, kidnappings are "black magic," while abductions are "white magic."

The very reason Western journalists get away with bad reporting about Haiti is the very reason Haiti is in the condition it is in—most Haitian leaders are either too indifferent or corrupt to care. If journalists publish something false about Haiti, there are no repercussions for them, their media house, or their country. With less than one percent of Haitians speaking English, most people are completely unaware of these derogatory reports, and even if they weren't, they wouldn't know the proper channels to contest them. According to Paul Farmer, former UN Deputy Special Envoy for Haiti, "Haiti's 'bad press' is bad indeed—not merely because it is defamatory... [but also] because it obscures Haiti's real problems, their causes, and their possible cures."[186] Journalists should be held to higher ethical standards in reporting.

As a schoolgirl growing up in Jamaica, I learned this little jingle, "What's in a name? A rose by any other name would smell just as sweet."

But as we'll see later on, words shape perceptions, and perceptions shape reality. How Haiti is portrayed in international media affects how foreigners view Haiti, which, in turn, has a significant impact on the posture they take coming into humanitarian encounters. If they view Haitians as helpless and incompetent, they will fail to include them in the planning and execution of projects which will inevitably lead to poor collaboration and many failed projects.

In the next chapter, we will turn our attention to the foreign aid apparatus in Haiti and how it has impacted the development of the country.

CHAPTER 7: FOREIGN AID IN HAITI

"Manje ou renmen, se li ki gonfle w"
(The food you love most can give you indigestion).
—Sometimes, the things we love can make us sick.

Why does Haiti remain poor despite receiving so much foreign aid? This is a multi-faceted question, but a major part of the answer is the motivations donors have for giving aid.

Instrumental Philanthropy

Bilateral aid may be defined as transactions undertaken by a donor country directly with an aid recipient.[187] According to Malik (2018), it is self-evident that wealthy countries do not disburse foreign aid primarily for humanitarian reasons based on the fact that not one of the five poorest countries in the world is among the top ten recipients of British or US aid. Instead, recipients are chosen for commercial and geopolitical reasons.

The main objective of bilateral foreign aid is often to strengthen export markets and support the expansion of domestic firms into the recipient economy. As such, donors "tie" over 50 percent of their aid so that recipients must use it to buy donor goods and services.[188] This is called "instrumental philanthropy," where donor countries satisfy their domestic business constituents while maintaining a humanitarian image for the international community.[189] As a result, research has found that in the long run, a donor country's exports to the recipient country increase by $2.15 for every dollar in aid given.[190] This concept is called a "transfer paradox" in which "foreign aid can be donor-enriching and recipient-immiserizing."[191] Yet it directly corroborates the biblical principle that "it is more blessed to give than to receive" (Acts 20:35).

The USAID (2020) website states explicitly that, first and foremost, its work "advances US national security and economic prosperity." This is a more politically correct version of its previous *raison d'être*, which was removed from its website in 2006: "The principal beneficiary of America's foreign assistance programs has always been the United States. Close to 80 percent of the US Agency for International Development's contracts and grants go directly to American firms."[192] Foreign aid has "created new markets for American industrial exports and meant hundreds of thousands of jobs for Americans."[193]

The donor interest model of foreign aid asserts that donor countries also use foreign aid as a political tool to advance their own interests in the following ways: to leverage power over the recipient country by exacting conditions in return for aid; by using the threat of aid termination to force compliance to various demands; to strengthen their bargaining position when the recipient requests debt-restructuring; and, foreign aid gives the donor power and access to intervene in the recipient's domestic affairs.[194]

As a Bangladeshi politician warned the newly independent fledgling nation that while they needed foreign aid, they must:

Exercise with circumspection and delicacy the power it puts into the hands of donors... Not all attempts to intervene are well-intentioned... and a country so heavily dependent on aid as Bangladesh can be made to suffer or to conform if there is a divergence of view between those who give and those who receive.[195]

If foreign aid recipients sense that poverty alleviation is not the priority of foreign aid donors, this may affect how aid recipients perceive foreign aid and foreign aid donors. "Recipients tend to emphasize the benefits of aid to donors and to ridicule the notion that it might be altruistic."[196] If aid recipients sense that there is an ulterior motive behind aid donors' charity, then this may engender resentment and cause aid recipients to intentionally or unintentionally sabotage aid interventions.[197] This reaction, in turn, affects foreign aid effectiveness and economic development.

US Aid and Haitian Politics

The United States is Haiti's largest foreign aid donor and headquarters to 51 percent of NGOs operating in Haiti.[198] According to Haiti experts, Ramachandran and Walz (2015), "Poverty reduction was always a secondary goal in the disbursement of foreign aid; assistance was primarily used as a reward or punitive measure to influence Haitian politics."[199]

Donor nations' political agendas, in addition to other factors, made foreign aid to Haiti very unpredictable. The volatility of foreign aid flows undermined the Haitian government's ability to create long-term plans for economic development. What little social progress was made during the years of high aid flows was reversed during the years when there was little. When humanitarian aid experienced relative stability, it funded mainly short-term relief projects that often dwarfed long-term development projects.[200]

Food Aid

USAID gives a lot of humanitarian aid to Haiti in the form of food. However, for the most part, political agendas have determined the outcome of these projects. Periods when there was a complete cessation of foreign aid and trade for political reasons had devastating long-term effects on Haiti's economic development, notably the 1991 US embargo in which imports of seeds and fertilizers were also blocked.[201] This event coincided with a "neoliberal economic program 'on steroids'"[202] in which the Haitian government was forced to cut its tariffs on American rice in the late 1980s from 35 percent to 3 percent while the US increased its subsidies to rice farmers exporting to Haiti.[203] As Haiti's agricultural sector lay in ruins, international NGOs swooped into the "rescue," often sending food aid (mainly US rice) which some say is equivalent to "dumping."[204] This combination of measures decimated Haiti's vibrant rice industry, which Oxfam, a leading international aid agency, reports was "virtually self-sufficient" in 1980.[205]

The United States spends more money on subsidizing its own rice farmers than it spends on aid to Haiti. The international organization Oxfam estimates that the US spends about $350 million on aid to Haiti, with a little over $22 million devoted to Haitian agriculture. It spends about $430 million each year subsidizing its rice farmers.[206]

Haiti now imports up to 80 percent of its rice (mainly from the United States) and about 60 percent of its general food supply.[207] US president Bill Clinton, who was instrumental in orchestrating US subsidies for rice exports to Haiti, later confessed that these subsidies were "a mistake."[208] Clinton further revealed that:

It may have been good for some of my farmers in Arkansas, but it has not worked...I have to live every day with the consequences of the lost capacity to produce a rice crop in Haiti to feed those people, because of what I did.[209]

He went on to become co-chair of the post-earthquake reconstruction efforts, which some considered to be a glaring conflict of interest in light of his previous involvement in the country.[210]

The United States is the largest food aid donor to developing countries. Based on the 1954 Public Law (PL) 480, the main objective of US food aid was to create an outlet for agricultural surplus and stabilize domestic food prices while creating a positive public image for America. The US government subsidizes its farmers by purchasing food at market prices then dumping the surplus onto the international market.[211] As such, economist Dobransky (2015) concludes that the interests of US domestic institutions are at "the forefront of food aid motivations."[212] Furthermore, though food aid is seemingly "humanitarian, soft, benign," prolonged food assistance has devastating long-term consequences, chief of which is accelerated population growth in poor countries leading to a depletion of scarce resources and a crippling of the recipient's agricultural industry.[213]

Dobransky (2015) suggests replacing food aid with other types of assistance that would improve the recipients' lives in the long run. Where food aid is used, it should be supplemented with economic aid that would encourage socioeconomic growth and the development of local agriculture. The author also urged policymakers to "remove any type of unnatural and unfair competition from foreign food suppliers" in order to give the agricultural sectors of recipient countries a fighting chance at survival.[214]

In light of the negative long-term effects food aid can have on the recipient country's economy, the reality of millions of people worldwide dying from lack of food presents a great dilemma. It calls for delicacy and discernment between situations where urgent relief is needed (such as in the case of natural disasters, war, and other manmade crises) and when development is needed to address more than the symptoms of poverty but the root cause.

Foreign Aid as an Engine of Development

Meds and Foods for Kids is a great example of how foreign aid donors can turn local production and job creation into a motor that powers local food relief programs. Founded in 2003, this organization educates Haitian farmers, buys their produce (peanuts), uses the peanuts to make therapeutic food for malnourished children, and exports surplus products to sixteen other countries. So far, they have nourished more than 530,000 infants back to health and trained more than 2,500 farmers. They employ close to 90 people at their factory. According to their website, "Our long-term vision sees a local economy in Haiti that grows and flourishes on its own, providing stable jobs and meeting the nutritional needs of every Haitian."[215]

At the government level, the Taiwanese-Haitian partnership is another success story of foreign aid at work to reduce hunger sustainably. This initiative (REPONSE-NNE) began in 2019 to increase rice production by teaching better cultivation techniques and producing and distributing pure varieties of rice seeds. They also provide credit to farmers, which covers the cost of seeds, plowing the fields, fertilizers, insecticides and herbicides, and labor. In return, the farmers sell REPONSE-NNE at least 70 percent of their produce, and they repay their debt in seeds.

In addition, REPONSE-NNE has built several multi-service agricultural support centers for rice farmers. These centers have all the farmers' need for rice production, such as technical expertise, tractors, tools, a rice mill, and bagging facilities. The centers are run by people from the community who are trained to do so. As a result of this project, rice production has increased from less than two tons per hectare to over five tons. So far, more than 5,800 people have benefitted directly from this project, and local rice production has increased substantially.

In the following chapter, we will zero in specifically on foreign aid after the 2010 earthquake. How much was donated, and where did it all go?

84

CHAPTER 8: FOREIGN AID AFTER THE 2010 EARTHQUAKE

"Fòk ou konn manje pawòl pou ou gen zanmi"
(You must be willing to apologize to keep a friend).

Where Did All the Money Go?

Ramachandran and Walz (2015), in their article "Haiti: Where Has All the Money Gone?" systematically researched and presented grim findings of foreign aid in Haiti after the 2010 earthquake. The earthquake caused damages estimated at $7.8 billion, well in excess of Haiti's GDP in 2009. In an unprecedented show of support and solidarity, private and official donations tripled between 2009 and 2010, amounting to more than 400 percent of state domestic revenues in 2010. Public sector donors pledged a total of $8.4 billion for relief and recovery efforts in 2010-2011 and disbursed $5.3 billion. The United States was the largest donor. The government pledged $3.2 billion, of which $1.9 billion was disbursed, while private donations rose to $3.1 billion. Sixty percent of US government aid was in the form of grants, while 40 percent was in the form of goods or services.[216] In all, Haiti has received a total of $13 billion in foreign aid since the 2010 earthquake.[217]

CLAUDIA CHARLOT

Haitian Government Bypassed

Foreign aid disbursements followed "the pattern of troubled relations between Haiti and the United States."[218] In most cases, the donors' agenda contradicted the Haitian government's priorities and funding requests. For example, pledges for the transportation sector ($737 million) were 510 percent more than what the government requested, while the government's request for $750 million for reconstruction was met with only $50 million in pledges and actual disbursements.[219]

Meticulously following the paper trails, Ramachandran and Walz (2015) found that "humanitarian agencies, NGOs, private contractors, and other non-state service providers received 99 percent of humanitarian aid—*less than 1 percent went to the government of Haiti*."[220] This amount was "barely more than [what] the government of the Dominican Republic [received], which hardly even felt the quake."[221]

According to Ramachandran and Walz (2015), the reason the Haitian government basically received none of the $1.28 billion in US humanitarian aid disbursed at the time of publication is the assumption that it lacked the capacity and was too corrupt to manage any funds. Instead, funds were channeled through the donors' own contractors and other international NGOs—an approach that is rife with its own drawbacks. Chief of these drawbacks is the "trickle down" effect in which foreign aid goes through multiple layers of subgrantees, each of which takes 7 to 10 percent in administrative fees, significantly reducing the amount available for the actual projects.[222]

The main recipients of foreign aid disbursements after the earthquake were US government agencies (such as the Department of Defense (DOD), the Federal Emergency Management Agency (FEMA), and Health and Human Services (HHS)); large international nonprofits and some UN agencies. Private contractors also benefitted considerably in what leaked cables described as a "gold rush."[223] Ramachandran and Walz (2015) revealed that the top ten private contractors were US-based, while Haitian-based NGOs were largely excluded from the reconstruction efforts, receiving only $9 million for contracts (less than 1 percent of more than a billion dollars spent by USAID). More disturbing is the fact that several US organizations which received multi-million-dollar contracts for work in Haiti had been embroiled in controversies pertaining to financial accountability and project outcomes in Iraq, Afghanistan, or Hurricane Katrina relief. These include Chemonics (the largest recipient of USAID contracts in Haiti) and FEMA. Since almost all the post-earthquake aid went to large international NGOs, one thing is clear, it was not the Haitian government that stole or mismanaged this money.

Bypassing the recipient country's government and indigenous organizations during relief efforts has been shown to perpetuate endemic poverty by undermining institutional capacity in developing economies. The international community's *de facto* support of NGOs instead of the Haitian government "made institution building unsustainable and compounded, instead of reducing, problems of government accountability to the electorate."[224]

Haiti has more NGOs than any other country in the region. In the next chapter, we will take a closer look at some factors that have impeded the efforts of these organizations.

CHAPTER 9: REPUBLIC OF NGOs

"Pa bay chat veye bè" (Don't ask a cat to watch the butter).

—Don't put a self-interested person in charge of valuable resources.

Multilateral Aid

Multilateral aid is classified as contributions of international agencies and organizations to an aid recipient.[225] Many governments deliver aid through NGOs because of these organizations' perceived strengths, including "their ability to reach the poorest and neediest recipients... [they are] cost-effective due to their lack of large bureaucracies... [and] their years of experience and level of expertise in developmental and relief work."[226]

In 1981, the US Congress mandated that a minimum of 13.5 percent of the country's aid budget be allocated to NGOs. USAID has exceeded this amount in recent years by allocating over 30 percent of its total budget to NGOs.[227]

While research has shown that many bilateral donors have ulterior motives for giving aid, it is generally assumed that NGOs are autonomous, nonpartisan actors working solely in the interests of the poor. However, economist Keck (2015) found that US NGO state-funded aid allocations mirror official US foreign aid. In essence, the US, as principal, has developed effective control mechanisms to ensure that officially funded NGOs undertake projects focused on their government's national security, political, and economic interests rather than the needs of the recipients. "This implies that US-funded NGO aid has an economic purpose, including assisting US businesses in gaining a greater share of the market in these states."[228] This has considerable implications for economic development and self-sufficiency in developing countries.

Lack of NGO Accountability

NGOs form a powerful "parallel state"[229] in Haiti, providing about 70 percent of healthcare and 85 percent of education.[230] Yet they operate with little government oversight, inter-agency coordination, or financial accountability. Thus, "bypassing the state, arguably to avoid corruption, presents a classical catch-22 situation."[231] Haitians call this "asking a cat to safeguard butter from a rat." According to a report on the accountability and transparency of NGOs working in Haiti one year after the earthquake, only eight out of 196 organizations identified had public and regularly updated reports on their activities in Haiti. "Almost 65 percent of organizations had no reports available, and instead provided emotional appeals or anecdotal case studies on their websites."[232]

Private NGOs are not the only entities that lack accountability. Surprisingly, "an external review of USAID's activities in Haiti lacks data completely, and there is very little in the report on accountability with regard to aid flows."[233] As the opening note from a USAID report aptly states

We had hoped to invest greater efforts in measuring more accurately the quality of aid and its impact on beneficiaries. However, a disquieting lack of data on baselines against which to measure progress or even impact forced this task to the back burner.[234]

USAID further states on its website,

Unfortunately, the Agency does not have the systems in place to track sub-grants and sub-contracts so it is not possible to state precisely the number of partners or the percentage of USAID funds that flow to local nonprofit organizations (or, for that matter, to local private businesses) through these indirect arrangements.[235]

Managing Poverty

According to anthropologist and Haiti expert Timothy Schwartz (2017), by and large, foreign NGOs have a vested interest in keeping Haiti poor and portraying things as worse than they are. Many foreign aid professionals, both Haitians and foreigners, build their careers on the existence of poverty and so have a vested interest in Haiti remaining poor. Managing poverty is big business. "An unjust social order is the permanent fount of this 'generosity,' which is nourished by death, despair, and poverty. That is why the dispensers of false generosity become desperate at the slightest threat to its source."[236]

A former World Bank official who worked on several projects in Haiti asked the same question that Ramachandran and Walz (2015) and many others have asked since the 2010 earthquake, "Where did the money go?" to which he surmised:

> On looking around Port-au-Prince, you do not see much sign of the US$12 billion-plus that has allegedly been poured into Haiti since the earthquake. However, there is one immediate sign of where a lot of the aid money has gone: Pajeros. Or Land Cruisers or Pathfinders take your pick, but Port-au-Prince's narrow streets are jammed with big SUVs emblazoned with an alphabet soup of NGO logos. There are 560 registered NGOs active in Haiti; and that does not include the multilateral donor agencies, development agencies, UN agencies, diplomatic staff, or church groups—the place is awash with well-intentioned white people! (Samuel, 2013, para. 23).

Unfortunately, most of the money donated for humanitarian aid in Haiti goes to wealthy expats to maintain their luxurious lifestyles. The rest is paid to foreign contractors who charge grossly inflated fees for their services. As such, the money does not get to those who need it the most—the poor and destitute.[237]

The Red Cross is one of the most shocking examples of this misappropriation of funds. In response to the earthquake, it pioneered text message donations raising an unprecedented $32 million in $10 donations by this method alone.[238] However, numerous investigations later revealed that though the Red Cross had raised half a billion dollars for Haiti, it built only six houses.[239] According to the report which exposed the Red Cross, the main reason for this gross mismanagement of funds was "an overreliance on foreigners who could not speak French or Creole."[240] While the Haitian government does have corruption, "what is striking in the matter are the double standards applied when differentiating state from international structures."[241]

Haitian Perceptions of NGOs

Development experts, Klarreich and Polman (2012), found that most international NGOs totally disregarded local institutions and followed their own agendas from beginning to end in their post-earthquake relief efforts. This disregard for local capacity led to many abandoned projects after the humanitarian teams left. Additionally, Logistic Base, the United Nations headquarters for the earthquake recovery efforts, was akin to "a luxury resort, totally inaccessible to the average Haitian citizen."[242] Stark contrasts between the living conditions of local aid donors and aid recipients have been known to contribute to animosity and impair mutual understanding between the two groups.[243] Klarreich and Polman (2012) also found that

> Almost two-thirds of the rest of the money raised—in the billions—remains in the bank accounts of the aid money managers that were there before the quake: internation-

al NGOs, the World Bank, the UN, the Inter-American Development Bank and mostly Western building and consultancy firms.[244]

In light of the post-earthquake response, "a growing number [of Haitians] have begun thinking of aid workers as thieves at best, colonizers at worst."[245] The lack of transparency and volatility of services has bred much distrust of NGOs in Haiti. "Haitians are, in general, not very happy with the international community. NGOs are variously described in Haitian Creole as 'volè' (thieves or crooks), 'malonèt' (liars), and 'kowonpi' (corrupt)."[246]

Given that NGOs and private contractors will continue to play a major role in Haiti for the foreseeable future, Ramachandran and Walz (2015) made three policy recommendations. First, NGOs and private contractors need to make comprehensive reports of their operations available to the public. Second, they need to become part of the International Aid Transparency Initiative by making their financial data available. Finally, the Haitian government should award contracts only after a public bidding process.

Disaster Tourism

Another aspect of NGO operations in Haiti that affects local perceptions is the photography and media coverage NGOs use for sensitization and fundraising purposes. In a poignant 1951 poem encapsulating "the issue of tourism, poverty, and the foreigner's gaze in Haiti," renowned Haitian poet and playwright Felix Morisseau-Leroy penned the following.

> Tourist, don't take my picture/Don't take my picture, tourist/I'm too ugly/Too dirty/Too skinny/Don't take my picture, white man/Mr. Eastman won't be happy/I'm too ugly/I'm gonna crack your Kodak/Don't take my picture, tourist/Leave me be, white man ... Tourist, don't take a picture of the house/My house is of straw/Don't take a picture of my hut/My hut's made of earth...Tourist, don't take my picture/ You don't understand my position/You don't understand anything/About my business, tourist/'Gimme fie cents'/And then, be on your way, tourist.[247]

This poem reveals that many Haitians are self-conscious about having their photos taken without their permission and for purposes they are not aware of. Furthermore, they are wary that their poverty is being used to enrich or entertain others.

In his essay, Garland (2015) examines,

> [...] the visual rhetoric of the post-earthquake NGO industry in Haiti, and how it reflects a particular kind of contemporary tourism boom: "voluntourists" who go to Haiti for various lengths of time, document their activities by way of cell phones and digital cameras, and circulate those images on social media platforms.[248]

95

During his 2012 visit to Haiti, Garland (2015) observed that residents of Cité Soleil and other communities in Port-au-Prince explicitly objected to being photographed, either verbally or by turning their faces away. However, the power dynamic changed when their photo was taken while they were waiting in line to receive free health services. They accepted these unsolicited "photo-ops" despite often appearing uncomfortable. These photos are "commoditized" by foreign NGOs and breach the "ethics of representation" since they are often taken without the subject's consent.[249]

In their editorial, "Haiti Disaster Tourism—A Medical Shame," Van Hoving, Wallis, Docrat, and De Vries (2010) made similar remarks. They were part of a South African-Mexican team of doctors and medical practitioners who came one week after the 2010 earthquake in Haiti. From their experience there, they made a critical distinction between the humanitarian healthcare worker who genuinely desires to help those in need, and the "disaster tourist" who is "a person heading to the site of a disaster to see the destruction, take pictures, obtain bragging rights, and get the shoulder badge."[250] They offered candid advice to those who want to help after disasters: "Put yourself in the victim's shoes" and "leave the media at home." For those who "crave media attention and the world's spotlight, do disaster victims a favor and stay at home."[251]

So far, we have heard from numerous experts about foreign aid in Haiti. In the following chapter, we will hear directly from the true experts on foreign aid in Haiti—the aid recipients themselves.

CHAPTER 10: EMPIRICAL RESEARCH

"Moun ki pase maladi konn remèd"
(Someone who was sick knows the cure).
—The person who went through a difficult situation is the best person to ask for advice.

After conducting extensive research of the literature pertaining to how foreign aid donors and Haitians perceive each other, I undertook empirical research to better understand what Haitians think about foreign aid donors and themselves. This is important because "Any attempt to improve the effectiveness of aid... lies in a complete rethinking of not just the policy agendas associated with aid but in the nature of the relationship between donors and recipients."[252]

Numerous studies have shown that how aid recipients feel about aid and aid donors can affect how aid recipients feel about themselves and their ability to ameliorate their own deplorable condition.[253] Therefore, it is important to find out what the poor themselves think about their predicament and the interventions that have been undertaken on their behalf in the name of poverty alleviation.

I conducted research into foreign aid recipient perceptions using the semi-quantitative approach, Q Methodology. Participants were given fifty cards with a variety of statements about foreign aid, foreign aid donors, and Haitians (Appendix 2). They were asked to arrange these on a grid or game board based on how much they agreed or disagreed with the opinions expressed on the cards. See Appendix 3 for the grid and Appendix 4 for an example of a completed game board. Thirty-five Haitian foreign aid recipients from seven different demographic groups participated in the research. After statistical analysis, the results revealed three distinct groups of perspectives Haitians have about foreign aid, foreign aid donors, and themselves.

Eighteen participants (51 percent) were part of Group 1 (Optimists), twelve (34 percent) were in Group 2 (Patriots), and two (6 percent) in Group 3 (Foreign Aid Advocates). Three respondents (9 percent) did not correlate strongly with any of the main groups (Figure 6).

Figure 6: Research results

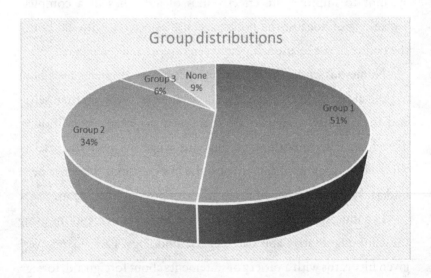

Description of Research Results

Following are the in-depth descriptions of each group with the actual statements respondents made during the exit interviews presented in quotation marks. Some key perspectives overlap between groups. The name given to each group describes their predominant trait but does not necessarily mean these characteristics are mutually exclusive. Finally, the main distinguishing statements will be used to highlight how people in these groups differ the most in their points of view.

Group 1: "Die-Hard Optimists"

This group is characterized by the fact that they strongly agree that Haiti is endowed with rich natural resources; however, either because of a lack of expertise or lack of government interest, these resources are not being explored and utilized for the benefit of the country. The government does not value these resources, nor do they care about the people, and so the resources are being wasted. As such, Haiti remains poor. Among the natural resources, respondents cited were the rich soil, solar and wind energy, gold, petroleum, even uranium, and other key minerals used in manufacturing phones. Pointing to the colonial and postcolonial eras, members of this group argued that Haiti's natural resources are what has made it a target of historical exploitation at the hands of the Spanish (for gold), France (for cotton and other crops), and the US (gold and other minerals). In order for the country to develop, Haitians need the knowledge, skills, and equipment to take advantage of the country's natural resources.

This group strongly believes that "work is freedom" and generally displays strong work ethic and high self-esteem. Work provides self-respect and freedom from dependency. "Work gives you the strength to decide the direction of your own life. You are truly independent to choose how you want to spend your own money. When you are dependent on someone for money, you are a beggar. They can push you around." "Work helps to preoccupy your mind and keep you from envious, harmful thoughts towards others who may have more than you." Many people in this group believe that God ordained work from the Garden of Eden, and several quoted Scripture such as 2 Thessalonians 3:10, "The one who is unwilling to work shall not eat;" or the Creation account where God worked for six days and then rested for one day. "If you're free but can't provide for yourself, what's the point of being free?"

This group is very optimistic about Haiti's future. Their belief in hope for Haiti lies in their unwavering faith in God who can do the impossible, a new generation of Haitians who are educated and willing to work for change, and the success stories of other countries that were worse off than Haiti. "If Haitians decide to unite, to run the country well, to utilize the country's vast untapped natural resources for the benefit of all its citizens, then Haiti will change." They also believe people can succeed in Haiti if they work hard and that Haitians have the same intellectual capacity as foreigners because all people were created equal by God.

This group most strongly disagrees with the notion that Voodoo is the only thing Haitians are good at. Most respondents described the numerous Haitian successes in the domain of sports, music, and academia. They also proudly mentioned the fact that Haiti was the first Black country to win its independence and helped several Latin American countries[254] and even the United States[255] to gain their independence also. Others highlighted the accomplishments of the Haitian Diaspora, which are well documented in works such as *Ces Québécois Venus d'Haïti* [These Quebecers from Haiti].[256] They cited the lack of adequate resources as the main reason why many Haitians are not able to fully develop their potential locally. Some respondents pointed out that other countries also practice magic regardless of whether people call one "black magic" and the other "white magic." Others explained that saying Voodoo is the only thing Haitians are good at "would imply that Haitians are not intelligent and that those of us who succeed in life only did so because of magic."

They described the tenacity of many Haitian school children who walk for miles to go to school to learn on an empty stomach. "Haitian success is different from success elsewhere. Getting 60 percent on an exam here is like getting 90 percent elsewhere because of the many obstacles we have to surmount." They explained that this erroneous idea was propagated by foreign missionaries and locals who wanted to raise awareness while raising money. Some members of this group insisted that Voodoo is losing ground in Haiti because almost every community has an evangelical church, and many Haitians know nothing about magic.

People who belong to this group also strongly oppose the idea that foreigners are the only ones with the answer to Haiti's problems. On the contrary, they believe that a lot of Haiti's woes are due to oppression and exploitation from foreign countries since Haiti's independence until now. "If foreigners could change this country, they would have done it already." "Foreigners are only human. They're not God." They explained that the idea that only foreigners can fix Haiti has caused a lot of damage. It has made many Haitians lazy and made a lot of foreigners think they are superior to Haitians. "A lot of Haitians believe that if a foreigner does not run an organization, it will crumble. As such, even when foreigners hand over leadership to locals, the foreigners think they are still in charge."

The respondents acknowledged the fact that people and countries may sometimes find themselves in need of help from others; however, the onus is on the person or country itself to fix their own problems. "Each person has primary responsibility for himself. You can find yourself in need for help, but you are the one responsible for yourself. In the same way, the wellbeing of this country depends on its citizens." Furthermore, foreign aid donors can get tired of helping because they have their own problems too. As mentioned before, this group strongly believes in the importance of work, and this was identified as the primary means through which Haitians should lift their country out of poverty.

In general, this group believes that hope for Haiti lies in God, Haiti's untapped resources, its people, and their willingness to unite and work hard. Notably, four of the five middle-to-upper-class respondents, foreign NGO employees, and government employees were in this group. Table 1 gives the demographic breakdown of each group.

Table 1: Demographic breakdown for each group

	Optimists	Patriots	Foreign Aid Advocates	None
Haitian NGO directors	3	1	1	0
Seniors	2	3	0	0
Lower class	0	5	0	0
Middle-/Upper- class	4	0	0	1
Foreign NGO employees	4	1	0	0
Young people	1	1	1	2
Government employees	4	1	0	0
TOTAL	18	12	2	3

Group 2: "Die-Hard Patriots"

Members of this group are very proud of Haiti's accomplishment as the first Black nation to have a successful slave revolt and overturn foreign domination. This fact is known all over the world and earns Haiti international respect. Even though Haiti is underdeveloped, this achievement gives them a strong sense of national identity and pride. "As a small slave colony, the Haitian warriors under the leadership of Toussaint Louverture, defeated the greatest army of its time— Napoleon the Great. Not only that, but we helped other countries— even the United States—gain their independence."[257] They explained that winning their independence gave them the right to their own land and their own language. "We fought for our dignity and proved that all people, regardless of color, are created in the image of God."

Like members of Group one (Optimists), Patriots strongly believe that work is the key to independence and dignity. Work is both an obligation and a privilege. "Wherever you are, whatever your level of education, you can work." "As long as you're willing to work, you can escape poverty." They explained that when someone constantly depends on someone else, it causes the recipient to become lazy, retards their potential, and prevents them from becoming successful. "Constant dependency prevents you from flying with your own wings" because "He who finances, commands," so an aid recipient is never really free. "Work is the key to progress."

People in this group strongly disagree that foreigners respect Haitians. They explained that when Haitians go to other countries, foreigners humiliate them because Haiti is poor. As proof, they described the injustices and violence Haitian university students have endured in the Dominican Republic even though they pay exorbitant tuition fees, which help the Dominican Republic economy.

Members of this group also share the same stance as Optimists who strongly disagree that only foreign aid can help Haiti develop. Like those in group one, they also insisted that foreign aid donors are not God; therefore, Haitians should not put all their hope on them. They emphasized the need for personal responsibility: "If your house is dirty, you're the one who should sweep it." They also emphasized the need for Haitian leaders and citizens alike to play their part: "The day Haitians stop being selfish, the country will change." Additionally, "If the Haitian government invests in agriculture, Haiti would be able to produce enough food for its population and would not need to depend on foreign aid." They also explained that sometimes poverty is a mindset, so even if foreigners want to help, if Haitians do not want change, it will never happen. "If we need foreign help for everything, the country will never develop."

People in this group express a strong distrust of foreigners. They do not believe that foreigners are honest nor that NGOs have projects that create lasting change. They believe foreign aid donors have ulterior motives in the aid interventions they undertake in Haiti. For example, they explained that foreign aid donors keep a sizeable amount of the funds raised for Haiti for themselves. In addition, they believe that many new diseases are brought into the country by foreigners. Interestingly, this group strongly believes in the importance of education even though all the members of the lower class were part of this group. One respondent used her husband as an example of those who believe in the importance of education. Even though he is sixty-seven years old, he was getting ready to take the government exam to receive his high school diploma.

The two perspectives that Optimists and Patriots disagree the most about are first, whereas the Optimists (Group 1) believe that Haitians and foreigners can be good friends, the Patriots (Group 2) disagree. These groups also differ the most in their perceptions about Haitian intelligence vis-à-vis that of foreigners. Optimists strongly believe that Haitians are as intelligent as foreigners, while those in Group 2 slightly disagree.

Group 3: "Die-Hard Foreign Aid Advocates"

Only two people identified as Die-Hard Foreign Aid Advocates, a female high school student and a female Haitian NGO director who operates a sponsored primary school. This group has an overall positive view of foreigners and foreign aid interventions. They most strongly adhere to the perspective that foreign aid donors who build schools and orphanages are motivated primarily by their love for Haitian children. "Foreigners see that Haitian children are smart, so they put them in school." "Foreign aid donors love Haitian children because they take a lot of photos with them, give them gifts, and take them on trips."

Like those in Group one (Optimists), Foreign Aid Advocates strongly believe that Haiti is endowed with rich natural resources. This group also believes that foreign aid donors work in Haiti because they are compassionate and that Haitians and foreigners can be good friends. One respondent described several fulfilling, long-term relationships she has had with foreigners, one lasting for over fifty years.

Despite their confidence in foreign aid and foreign aid donors, this group strongly believes in the importance of working and saving regardless of whether one receives regular money transfers from overseas or not. They strongly disagree with those who rely completely on help from overseas. They explained that having personal savings is important because your foreign aid donor can lose their job or find themselves in some other difficulty and no longer support you. They cited the current COVID-19 pandemic as a case in point where many North Americans have lost their jobs and are no longer able to help their relatives and friends in Haiti or are not able to help as much. They also disagree that foreigners come to Haiti to exploit the country's resources or that people working in NGOs are only concerned about keeping their jobs.

Optimists and Foreign Aid Advocates differ the most on the subject of Haitian intelligence. Optimists strongly believe that Haitians are as intelligent as foreigners, while Foreign Aid Advocates strongly disagree. Additionally, while Optimists expressed slight agreement with the idea that many Haitians refuse to work because they get money from overseas, Foreign Aid Advocates strongly disagreed.

The biggest distinction between Foreign Aid Advocates and Patriots is that while the Foreign Aid Advocates strongly disagree that many Haitians refuse to work because they receive regular help from donors overseas, Patriots are basically neutral. Furthermore, while Patriots think foreigners come to Haiti to exploit its resources, Foreign Aid Advocates disagree.

A Missing Group: The "Die-Hard Pessimists"

Based on my experience in Haiti, one dominant group is missing from the data set. I would name this group the "Die-Hard Pessimists." For this group, there is nothing positive about Haiti, nothing to be celebrated, and nothing to be hopeful about. The outlook is bleak, and there is no prospect for improvement.[258] They frequently say, "People are evil" (*Lezòm mechan*), "Haiti is slippery ground" (*Ayiti tè glise*), and "Haiti is hell" (*Ayiti se lanfè*). Recently, as I waited in line at a Western Union office, the man in front of me complained to the cashier, "Haiti is not a country, it's just a place where people live." I have heard many colorful comments like that before. People in this group find something wrong with everything in Haiti. For example, in 2011, the government fixed a stretch of the main road near my house that was muddy when wet and billows of dust when dry. I was exuberant. But instead of seeing this as a positive sign of progress, some people retorted, "Why wasn't it fixed long ago?" Others said the asphalt was not thick enough or the road repairs were not long enough.

Pessimists tend to focus on Haiti's poverty and, as such, have low self-esteem. For example, as an English as a second language (ESL) teacher in Haiti, one of the most uncomfortable topics to teach over the years has been about meals and food groups. As I teach about the different foods people around the world eat for breakfast, lunch, and dinner, inevitably, some students would point out, "Not in Haiti. Here we're lucky if we get one meal." Recently, some university students made the same remark even though they have three square meals each day on campus. When discussing what foods are healthy and in what proportions, students would reply, "That doesn't apply in Haiti. Here we eat whatever we can find." I pointed out to them that being poor does not necessarily mean that Haitians eat more unhealthy foods than people in developed countries. Actually, the Haitian diet includes more organic, home-cooked meals and less processed foods than that of many other Western countries, which leads to fewer cases of "lifestyle diseases," such as diabetes and hypertension.[259] Fewer lifestyle diseases was cited by experts as one of the possible reasons Haiti has one of the lowest numbers of mortalities from COVID-19 in the region.[260] Yet, Die-Hard Pessimists tend to feel inferior because Haiti is poor. Pessimists would seize any opportunity to leave the country, which may be why they did not show up in the results. Maybe most of them have already left. Or maybe they are among the respondents (9 percent) who did not correlate strongly with any of the three main groups.

In chapter 11, we will draw together the findings from the literature and our research in order to make recommendations for the path forward.

CHAPTER 11: INTERPRETATION OF RESEARCH RESULTS

"Bat fè a lè li cho" (If you want to forge iron,
you must hammer it when it's hot).
—Seize the opportunity when the time is right.

While much research has been conducted on foreign aid effectiveness from an economic perspective, not much research has been done to ascertain the impact of foreign aid recipient perceptions on the effectiveness of foreign aid interventions and economic development. The research findings presented in this chapter will address this knowledge gap by providing critical insights into how Haitians perceive foreign aid, foreign aid donors, and themselves, and whether these perceptions have adversely affected self-efficacy, work ethic, and hence, economic development.

How Do Haitians Perceive Foreign Aid?

The results make it clear that many Haitians see foreign aid as necessary under dire circumstances, but their greatest desire is to be able to "stand on their own two feet" through gainful employment and utilizing their country's natural resources. The "love/hate" relationship with foreign aid is clear. Whereas Haitians acknowledge the usefulness of foreign aid, they also express fear and resentment about how their country's economic vulnerability puts them in a position of weakness and dependency on foreign aid donors. A

vast majority of respondents, particularly Optimists (Group 1) and
Patriots (Group 2) expressed this concern. These findings support
that of other researchers[261] who described help as a "mixed blessing."
This is because "Although recipients frequently view aid as a positive,
supportive act that reflects donor caring and concern, they may
also experience negative consequences including feelings of failure,
inferiority, and dependency."[262]

How Do Haitians Perceive Foreign Aid Donors?

The research revealed that there is a group of Haitians (Foreign Aid
Advocates) that have had mostly positive experiences with foreigners
and hold very positive views of foreign aid donors. However, others
think that while trying to help the country, some foreign aid donors
do harm by propagating false notions and exaggerating Haiti's
problems in order to raise funds (Optimists).

Another group of Haitians (Patriots) is wary of foreigners and
their motives for giving foreign aid. Haiti's turbulent history with
foreign countries and frequent tensions with neighboring Dominican
Republic contributes greatly to these perceptions. Furthermore,
the attitude foreign aid donors have towards foreign aid recipients
seems to have equal or greater importance than the aid itself. Both
Optimists and Patriots insist that foreigners do not have the ultimate
answers to Haiti's problems. They do not see foreign aid donors as
"saviors," which would suggest that they may resent if foreign aid
donors act otherwise.

Furthermore, Patriots strongly disagree that foreigners respect Haitians. This perception is based on negative experiences Haitians have had with foreigners. The most cited example was the difficulties Haitians face in the Dominican Republic. These perceptions may impact the interaction of Haitians with foreign aid donors and hence have serious implications for the outcome of humanitarian interventions. If foreign aid donors appear to have a "chip on their shoulder," some Haitians may fail to reciprocate aid indirectly through neglect or directly through sabotage, thus impacting economic development.

How Do Haitians Perceive Themselves?

Despite Haiti's economic setbacks, most of the respondents demonstrated a strong sense of national pride, firstly, from being the first Black republic to win its independence from a foreign colonizer (Patriots) and secondly, because of the outstanding accomplishments of the Haitian Diaspora (Optimists). They reminisce with pride on Haiti's glory days of wealth and political clout. However, they also lament Haiti's current deplorable situation and reproach their government for not really caring about the well-being of its people, which leaves the country vulnerable to foreign exploitation (Optimists).

How Does Receiving Foreign Aid Affect Self-Efficacy and Work Ethic in Haiti?

Self-efficacy is "related to holding more positive views of one's circumstances."[263] It may be defined as "people's beliefs in their capabilities to mobilize the motivation, cognitive resources, and courses of action needed to exercise control over task demands."[264] According to the Merriam-Webster dictionary, w*ork ethic* may be defined as "a belief in work as a moral good; a set of values centered on the importance of doing work and reflected especially in a desire or determination to work hard."[265]

In general, Haitians have high self-esteem, view themselves as having intrinsic value, and believe in their potential to make a significant contribution to the world if given the opportunity.

Overall, the results show that Haitians possess a strong work ethic and resilience in the face of daunting odds. This ethic is demonstrated by the fact that both Optimists and Patriots strongly believe that "Work is freedom." Regarding how receiving foreign aid affects self-efficacy and work ethic in Haiti, while some respondents opined that receiving foreign aid has made some Haitians lazy, for others, it has increased their determination to work hard in order to become financially independent.

Table 2 contains a summary of the most dominant perceptions (from -5 to -3 and +5 to +3) for each group.

Table 2: Summary of the most dominant perceptions for each group

	FACTOR 1: "Optimists"	FACTOR 2: "Patriots"	FACTOR 3: "Foreign Aid Advocates"
Perceptions about foreign aid	- Disagree that "Foreign aid helps reduce problems in Haiti." - Disagree that "Vaccines from NGOs are good."	- Quite strongly disagree that "NGOs have projects that create lasting change."	No dominant perceptions.
Perceptions about foreign aid donors	- Strongly disagree that "Only foreigners can fix Haiti's problems." - Quite strongly disagree that "Foreigners bring a lot of new diseases to Haiti."	- Strongly disagree that "Only foreigners can fix Haiti's problems." - Strongly disagree that "Foreigners respect Haitians."	- Strongly agree that "Aid donors build schools and orphanages because they love Haitian children." - Quite strongly disagree that "Only foreigners can fix Haiti's problems."

Perceptions about themselves and the country	- Strongly agree that "Haiti has a lot of natural resources." - Quite strongly agree that "There is hope for Haiti."	- Strongly agree with "I am proud that Haiti was the first Black republic in the world." - Quite strongly agree that "Haiti has a lot of natural resources."	- Strongly agree that "Haiti has a lot of natural resources." - Agree that "Haiti will always need foreign aid."
Self-efficacy	- Strongly disagree that "Magic is the only thing Haitians are good at." - Quite strongly agree that "Haitians are as intelligent as foreigners."	No dominant perceptions.	- Strongly disagree that "Many Haitians don't save because they get money from overseas." - Disagree that "Magic is the only thing Haitians are good at."

Work ethic	- Strongly agree that "Work is freedom." - Quite strongly agree that "You can succeed in Haiti if you work hard."	- Strongly agree that "Work is freedom." - Quite strongly disagree that "Many Haitians believe going to school is a waste of time."	- Strongly disagree that "Many Haitians don't work because they get money from overseas." - Quite strongly agree that "There are jobs some Haitians wouldn't do in Haiti, but they do overseas."

Note: Strongly agree/ disagree = score of +5/ -5

Quite strongly agree/ disagree = score of +4/ -4

Agree/ Disagree = score of +3/ -3

CHAPTER 12: SYMPOSIUM

"Mande chemen pa di pèdi pou sa"
(Asking for directions doesn't mean you're lost).
—Don't feel embarrassed to ask for help.

Following my research, I hosted a symposium on foreign aid and economic development in Haiti. This event was held at Emmaus University, Cap-Haitian, with a three-fold purpose: to triangulate my research, to publicly present the findings of my Q study, and to invite suggestions and recommendations about how foreign aid can be more effectively utilized in Haiti. Getting feedback from members of the public added credence to my research. The audience was made up of fifty-three undergraduate theology students, thirteen staff members, one master's student, and three outside guests. This symposium signaled hope for Haiti in the midst of a global pandemic. Haiti is one of very few countries in the western hemisphere where more than seventy people could gather together (in November 2020), closely seated in an enclosed space without fear of COVID-19 infection. Because of divine providence, Haiti's storyline did not play out as many expected.

Survey 1: Main Reasons Why Haiti Is Underdeveloped

Three surveys were conducted throughout the symposium. I conducted a pre-conference survey as the participants arrived. They were asked to write the three main reasons they think Haiti remains underdeveloped. The three major reasons identified were poor or corrupt leadership, disunity, and the need for educational reform. See Figure 7 for the complete survey results.

Figure 7: Main reasons why Haiti remains poor

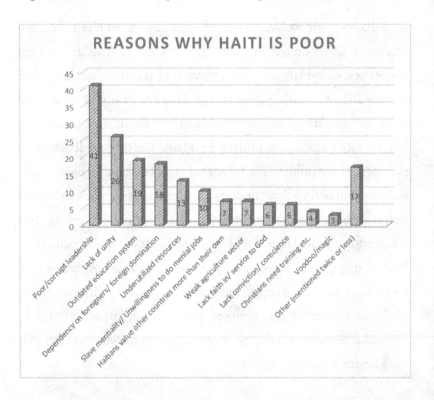

Survey 2: Choose One of the Three Factors

To begin my presentation, I gave an overview of Haiti, then condensed my literature review, focusing mainly on the economic and psychological theories about (foreign) aid. I then gave a simplified version of my research method and described the three resulting groups. At this point, I did a quick survey of the participants asking them to check on a piece of paper which group they most identify with. Forty-six people (71 percent) identified themselves as Optimists, nineteen (29 percent) as Patriots, and none as Foreign Aid Advocates. These results resembled those of my research.

It is very encouraging that many Haitians remain hopeful about the country's future. However, I had expected the results to be skewed in favor of foreign aid because the conference was held at a university owned by a Christian NGO, and all the students paid subsidized tuition fees. The reason for this result may be because the university is now led and staffed primarily by Haitians and may not be perceived as a "foreign" institution or maybe as an exception to the rule.

Group Discussions

Then five break-out groups were formed, each with ten to fifteen people to discuss firstly why they think Haiti has remained underdeveloped despite receiving a lot of foreign aid; and secondly, specific suggestions about how foreign aid can be better utilized for the development of Haiti. Table 3 presents a summary of their discussions.

Table 3: Group discussion results

	Q1. Why has Haiti remained underdeveloped despite receiving a lot of foreign aid?	Q2. Suggestions about how to better utilize foreign aid.
Group 1	• Foreign aid is a tool of neo-colonialism. • Haitians misuse foreign aid. • Haitians are stuck in a mindset of poverty. • The Haitian government is irresponsible. • Foreign countries give in order to keep the recipient country poor.	• Use foreign aid based on the needs of the Haitian people, not the needs of the donor country. • Create more jobs. • The Haitian government should ensure that those who need aid most receive it. • Invest in education.
Group 2	• Many NGOs are not legal because they are not registered with the Haitian government. • NGOs control all of the foreign aid funds, while the Haitian government receives none. • Most of the money NGOs receive is used to pay expatriates, so Haiti does not benefit.	• Create more jobs. • Invest in skills training. • Develop the agricultural sector. • Micro-finance for small and medium-sized enterprises.

Group 3	• Haiti needs foreign aid but also needs the institutional capacity to use it where it is needed most. • Most of the money NGOs receive is used to pay expatriates, so the money goes back to the donor countries.	• The Haitian government needs to tell the NGOs what and where the greatest needs are. • There needs to be local supervision of foreign aid to ensure that it serves the people.
Group 4	• Donor countries give too many conditions for the use of foreign aid. • Foreign aid is used to fix short-term problems. • Foreign aid creates dependency. • Foreign aid is not distributed properly. • Foreign aid donors have ways to get back the money they gave without the recipient knowing. • NGOs use poverty in Haiti to justify their existence.	• Invest in "grassroots" community development projects. • Invest in agriculture. • The Haitian people should determine how foreign aid is used, not foreign aid donors.

| Group 5 | • Foreign aid has a negative psychological impact on recipients. They think of aid as good luck, and so they waste it instead of seeing it as an opportunity to invest.
• Foreign aid donors give for selfish reasons because the aid is tied. | • Invest in a comprehensive educational system that includes personal development (self-esteem; national identity).
• Create new businesses.
• Haitians should have the philosophy that "Aid donors help me today so I can help someone else tomorrow..
• Haiti should transition from being an aid beneficiary to being an economic partner. |

The main reason the participants cited for Haiti remaining underdeveloped despite receiving foreign aid was that foreign aid goes back to donor countries either to pay expatriate salaries or to buy donor products. The most common suggestion about how to better utilize foreign aid was that the Haitian government and people should have more say in how foreign aid is used so that it can better serve their needs.

I ended the symposium with some preliminary conclusions and recommendations on how foreign aid can be more effectively utilized in Haiti. These recommendations include a comprehensive youth development program, which is detailed in Chapter 14. But first, I will discuss the mindset required to successfully implement community development programs in hard places like Haiti.

CHAPTER 13: GET YOUR HEAD IN THE GAME!

"Yo pa ranje tòl kay nan lapli"
(Don't wait for rain to fix a leaky roof).
—Don't wait until it's too late to prepare for disaster.

Few people understand the impact of perception on performance more than professional athletes do. How one perceives oneself and one's opponent or obstacle is a key determinant of whether one wins or loses.

> At all levels of sports—from pee-wees to the pros... the perception the athlete experiences actually triggers neurotransmitters ("fight or flight"), which in turn activate congruent behavioral responses... Perception, therefore, can be best understood as the trigger that determines whether the athlete will experience confidence or fear.[266]

The same principle applies to community development. How aid donors and recipients perceive each other, themselves, and the socioeconomic challenges in the community will impact the outcome of the humanitarian interventions. The right mindset is required for optimal performance.

Before proposing a viable option for moving Haiti from economic dependence to independence, I will explore two mental blocks that will undermine any community development game plan no matter how good: deficit-based community development and unhealthy dependency.

Deficit-Based Community Development

Numerous foreign aid experts have conceded that "It is clear that past aid solutions for Haiti, no matter how well-intentioned, have not worked."[267] It is my thesis that the main reason for this failure is because most foreign aid donors have adopted a deficit-based community development model due to their negative perceptions of Haiti fed by mass media. A deficit-based community development approach views troubled communities as "needy and problematic neighborhoods populated by needy and problematic and deficient people."[268] Deficit-based programs teach aid recipients "the nature and extent of their problems" and turn them into passive "consumers of services" or "client neighborhoods."[269]

But most importantly, a deficit or needs-based approach to community development is based on "the perception that only outside experts can provide real help."[270] This may lead to a clash of perceptions with Optimists and Patriots alike who strongly disagree that "Only foreigners can fix Haiti's problems." A Haitian psychologist who lives overseas and runs an orphanage in Port-au-Prince once shared how she came to visit Haiti a few years after the 2010 earthquake. The plane was almost full of short-term missionaries with t-shirts emblazoned "Rescue Haiti." She wondered with dry humor at how they expected to pull that off in two weeks!

A deficiency mindset causes many foreign aid organizations in Haiti to overlook local resources such as the intellectual capacity and creativity of Haitians.[271] This mindset leads to investing more in projects than in people. As one participant in my research so succinctly put it,

> Most foreign aid projects are not durable because aid donors don't invest in what can really bring lasting change-people. They focus more on material things than on people. Nor do they invest in projects that create sustainable jobs. Investing in people is the best investment you can make because only people can transform the environment we live in. So, the more you value people, the more you'll have a better environment. For example, building a park is good. But over time, it will fall apart. But if you train people, they can build even more beautiful parks.

Interestingly, this eloquent comment came from a member of the lower-income group who participated in my research.

Overlooking Haiti's rich local assets also means that many foreign aid donors also ignore other international organizations already on the ground. This "fragmentation of efforts"[272] is a major cause for humanitarian ineffectiveness in Haiti.[273]

Instead of focusing on a community's needs and deficiencies, Asset-Based Community Development (ABCD) and Appreciative Inquiry (AI) are two alternative community development strategies that draw attention to what works within a community. They are based on the assumptions that "in every society... something works" and "what we focus on becomes our reality."[274] Based on the results of my research, ABCD is the most ideal approach to socio-economic development in Haiti since the two main groups (Patriots and Optimists) look to the positive things about Haiti's past or present as inspiration for a better future.

Unhealthy Dependency

A World Bank study concluded that "Aid dependence and the interference of external governmental and nongovernmental actors [continue] to prevent Haiti from developing home-grown solutions and institutional capacity."[275] Haiti's only hope for development lies in urgently putting measures in place to become more economically independent. "The dependency syndrome has little to do with wealth or poverty. It has to do with a mentality on the part of both local people and the outsiders who try to help."[276]

Avoid Paternalism

To break unhealthy dependency, foreign aid donors should be mindful of several things. Firstly, they need to avoid paternalism. This is the tendency aid donors have "to take charge, particularly when it appears that nobody else is moving fast enough...[to] plan, manage, and direct initiatives in low-income communities when people in those communities could do those things quite well already."[277]

From the literature and my research, it is evident that many humanitarian interventions in Haiti are rife with paternalism. Some foreign aid donors, notoriously those on short-term trips,[278] tend to do projects Haitians could do or at least actively participate in. This is true, especially when it comes to projects involving manual labor that many Haitians would be eager to do for a small stipend. I would encourage foreign work teams to work alongside Haitians as much as possible in order to not inadvertently convey the message, in word or deed, that "We have to do it for you, because you can't." Because then they never will. Furthermore, paternalism may not sit well with Optimists who believe that "Haitians are as intelligent as foreigners" and Patriots who feel that "foreigners do not respect Haitians."

Paternalism is such a pervasive problem in community development circles that experts have sworn by this rule of thumb when working among the poor: "Never do for others what they can do for themselves."[279]

Actively Involve Aid Recipients

Secondly, in order to avoid unhealthy dependency, aid recipients must be actively involved in all stages of the intervention. Many foreign aid donors in Haiti fail to consult local leaders or residents in the design or execution of their projects[280] but forge ahead based on the notion that they possess superior intelligence. In their book, *When Helping Hurts*, community development experts Corbett and Fikkert observed that North Americans and people in the developing world "have internalized the messages of centuries of colonialism, slavery, and racism: Caucasians run things and everyone else follows...It is reflective of a god-complex to assume that we have all the knowledge and that we always know what is best."[281]

The tendency to exclude Haitians in designing and implementing projects is clearly off-putting to many Haitians since Optimists and Patriots demonstrate that they strongly believe in their intrinsic value and understand from history Haiti's capacity to thrive. Furthermore, failure to adequately involve Haitians in the design and implementation of foreign aid projects may be perceived as disrespectful, particularly by Patriots. While the patron-client culture may restrain many Haitians from openly expressing their displeasure with foreign aid donors' take-charge attitude, this disgruntlement may find other channels.

At the government level, tackling unhealthy dependency government is more complicated but even more crucial. "Capacity will never be built or improved if donors continue to bypass local institutions in favor of non-state actors."[282] Lack of government involvement not only undermines government legitimacy but engenders "indifference about the success or failure of programs."[283]

Evaluating foreign aid a decade after the 2010 earthquake, Haiti specialists agree that "international assistance was more effective when designed to cooperate with Haitians and plumb their ingenuity, know-how, and familiarity with the terrain than when provided from on high and designed to serve the donor nation's interests."[284]

Rethink Haiti

Effective foreign aid interventions must begin with rethinking Haiti. Both ABCD and measures to combat unhealthy dependency require a fundamental shift in how aid donors perceive the poor. Aid donors that view Haiti as powerless and pitiful should pull back the curtain on Haiti's history and keep it clearly in view as a testament to the potential of these people and the heights they can once again attain. Before systematic oppression from without and within broke the back of the Haitian civilization, it was a pioneer of Black leadership, Black literature, and Black legitimacy in the western hemisphere and indeed worldwide. For example, Haiti built the first skyscraper in the western hemisphere, the *Citadelle Henry*, in 1820. Made of limestone cemented by a mortar of lime and sand, its walls are as high as 160 feet and as thick as 16 feet. This extraordinary feat of engineering stands on the lofty summit of mount *Laferrière*, 3,000 feet above sea level, as a monument to the liberty of slaves everywhere.[285] It was Henry Christophe, Haiti's first King and the one who masterminded the Citadelle, who declared: "Too long has the African race been unjustly represented. Yet if we had even the names of our great men...if we could lay our hands on things we have made, monuments and towers and palaces, we might find our strength and our pride in terms white men as well as black men can understand."[286]

Discipleship Evangelical Church, which my husband and I planted in 2012, is a good example of what can be achieved when people rethink Haiti. More than half of our 350 members are unemployed high school and university students, and the adult employment resembles that of the general Haitian population. Despite this, we embarked on an ambitious project in 2016 to raise US$75,000 to buy land. We encouraged everyone, no matter how "poor," to give their best gift based on the principle that "It is more blessed to give than receive." Importantly, we led by example. After two years, we raised more than the required amount, with only 25 percent coming from overseas.

Relief vs. Development

At this point, an important distinction must be made between relief and development. "'Relief' can be defined as the urgent and temporary provision of emergency aid to reduce immediate suffering from a natural or man-made crisis."[287] Anyone can be unexpectedly in need of help in a crisis, and it is incumbent upon those who can, to help. After the crisis, however, it is important that efforts to help are geared toward development, which has as its goal to enable recipients to work and support themselves and their families with the fruits of their labor.[288]

Bearing in mind that "local populations are unlikely to feel a personal attachment to a solution externally imposed unless actively consulted or involved in the intervention strategy,"[289] the following community development strategy should involve foreign aid recipients at every stage of the intervention—from fundraising to design to implementation. In terms of fundraising, I would encourage foreign aid donors to involve the Haitian Diaspora and network with local businesses to encourage them to give back to their communities by financing specific projects.

This ongoing dialogue and cooperation are well-needed to rebuild local trust in NGOs.[290] Additionally, this approach will capitalize on the inherent trust Foreign Aid Advocates have for NGOs while meeting the intrinsic need for respect expressed by Patriots.

In the following chapter, I will elaborate on a comprehensive youth development program that can effectively utilize foreign aid to spur Haiti's long-term economic development.

CHAPTER 14: HEALTHY AID

"Bondye pa bay pitit Li penn san sekou" (God never gives His children a problem without giving them a solution).

Since they have not as yet experienced as many failures and disappointments as adults, young people usually possess a unique willingness to try to solve old problems and to create new opportunities. This fresh perspective and ability to remain undaunted by past failures are qualities that can make a young person an ideal entrepreneur.[291]

Fifty-five percent of Haitians are under age of twenty-four.[292] Haiti's young population represents the biggest opportunity for Haiti to be transformed. Many Haitians agree. Optimists believe that a new generation of educated, hard-working young people is one of the greatest sources of hope for Haiti. If this opportunity is seized through education, skills training, environmental awareness, small business development, and biblical and sexual education, I strongly believe that Haiti can be completely transformed within one generation.

Academics and Skills Training

My husband, Guenson, is a testament to the difference investing in a young person's education can make and the impact that it can have on an entire community. As the youngest of nine children from a poor, rural family, he was the only one who completed high school. For five years afterward, he could not continue his education because his parents, who were small-scale farmers, could not afford it. Nor could he find a job, but he kept himself busy by volunteering at Campus Crusade for Christ. On an ordinary day, totally unaware that he was being observed, an African American missionary came up to him and said, "I realize that you are good soil. I'm going to plant a seed in your life." And so, he sent him to Jamaica to a small Bible college to do a diploma in Theology. From there, he graduated valedictorian and was awarded a scholarship to complete a bachelor's degree in New Brunswick, Canada. From there, he received a scholarship to do a master's in Jackson, Mississippi. After that, he did two years' Ph.D. study in Britain, then completed his doctoral program in the United States. He is now president of Emmaus University,[293] an institution founded by American missionaries fifty-five years ago. His story is inspiring a new generation of young Haitians to dream big.

It was John F. Kennedy who declared, "Our progress as a nation can be no swifter than our progress in education. The human mind is our fundamental resource."[294] NGOs are already doing a tremendous job in Haiti's educational system. I would encourage them to continue investing in education which, based on the results of my empirical study and symposium, is the most favorable contribution being made by foreign aid donors. Haitians greatly value education. One senior citizen from the lower class explained: "I can't read or write because my parents didn't send me to school. They didn't know any better, nor could they afford it. But I sent all my children to school because that's the way to succeed in life."

While many educational NGOs sponsor students, others like the Canadian NGO Joy and Hope of Haiti, sponsor schools directly by covering a part of the teachers' salaries. They also have feeding programs and school gardens, which supplement the feeding program while teaching students agricultural skills.

In terms of curriculum, NGOs in Haiti's educational sector should place more emphasis on mathematics, English, information technology, and the sciences. I would also encourage, in addition to academics, that NGOs include alternative paths to success in their educational programs. These programs may include technical skills training, sports, and the visual and performing arts. In addition, I would encourage foreign aid donors who are passionate about education to adopt a public school in Haiti. Most public schools are in extreme disrepair and are desperately understaffed. These schools are where Haiti's poorest children receive their education. This considerable inequity between public and private school education helps to perpetuate Haiti's rigid, polarized social class structure, which has been at the root of constant social upheavals.[295] To upend this vicious cycle, foreign aid donors can invest in extracurricular activities, food programs, school kits, scholarships, and summer camps for outstanding students in public schools.

Importantly, Haitian students should not only be equipped with book knowledge and technical skills, but as one group at the symposium pointed out, they should also be taught civic duty and nationalism. They should be given a different vision for the future of their country and their part in it.

Finally, education plays a large part in shaping the perceptions of the next generation. While it is important to teach children in former colonies their country's history of oppression, Haitian parents and educators should be careful to avoid the extremes of a victim mentality or reverse racism. According to the symposium participants, a victim mentality or slavery mindset is one of the main reasons why Haiti remains underdeveloped (See Figure 7). This mindset is accompanied by feelings of helplessness, pessimism, and shame.[296] *Reverse racism* may be defined as "Prejudice, discrimination, or antagonism on the basis of race directed against a member of a dominant or privileged racial group."[297] This mindset of antagonism, on the other hand, perpetuates anger and resentment against former colonial masters, which keeps the former colony stuck in the past and unable to seize present opportunities.

Business Training and Micro-Finance

Lewis is a young tailor living in rural Haiti. With a small business loan, he was able to buy much-needed materials and pay three employees. With money from his tailor shop, he was able to pay his school fees and complete his final year of high school. He lives with and supports his younger brother, who is currently in high school.[298]

According to Abraham Maslow, "The most valuable 100 people to bring into a deteriorating society would not be economists, or politicians, or engineers, but rather 100 entrepreneurs."[299] However, owners of small and medium-sized enterprises find it particularly difficult to get access to credit in Haiti. Lack of credit limits their ability to take advantage of opportunities, grow, and create employment. The Haitian banking sector is highly concentrated, with the three largest banks controlling close to 80 percent of the industry's assets. In addition, 10 percent of individual borrowers receive nearly 80 percent of total loans. Nearly 40 percent of total credit goes to commerce and services activities, while agriculture receives less than 0.2 percent.[300]

One success story of innovative foreign aid intervention in Haiti has been micro-finance.[301] A micro-loan is all the chance many people need to lift themselves out of poverty. Hand-Up Micro Credit,[302] which I manage, is one example of how a small loan can make a big difference for a Haitian entrepreneur. It was founded in 2018 by a group of American Christian businessmen who wanted to go beyond offering a business training program. With an initial investment of only $10,000, we have disbursed 706 loans to date of on average $115 each. In our first year, we had a 92 percent repayment rate, and after the global pandemic and political upheavals, 87 percent.

Haitians are extremely entrepreneurial and enterprising. From the results of this research, Optimists believe that "You can succeed in Haiti if you work hard," and both Optimists and Patriots strongly believe that "Work is freedom." Business training, micro-credit combined with business coaching can ignite this potential and create an explosion of creativity and job creation. I encourage more NGOs to consider becoming involved in projects like these in Haiti.

> For the international development community, Haiti promises to be an interesting test case to see if grassroots entrepreneurial and technology-driven private development solutions will help break the development logjam... Most essential is the development of the local economy and jobs for the chronically underemployed Haitian population...[303]

One innovative business model that could specifically address Haiti's social needs while avoiding unhealthy dependency is a social business. A social business is a "non-loss, non-dividend company devoted to solving a social problem."[304] It is owned either by investors who reinvest all the profits or by the poor themselves. Social business is an innovative way to invest in foreign aid. Traditionally, aid funds are quickly depleted, leaving the NGO in constant need to raise more but investing this money in a social business would generate revenue for ongoing development projects while creating employment. This is sustainable development.

Environmental Programs

The World Bank's *What a Waste* study reveals that cities generate about 1.3 billion tons of solid waste a year.[305] Experts predict that due to mass rural-urban migration in developing countries like Haiti, the amount of waste being generated in cities will double in the near future.

Improper garbage disposal across Haiti is not only creating a public health hazard but is threatening to destroy this island paradise's most valuable resources—its air, land, and sea. Garbage strewn across the streets and clogging canals eventually ends up on the beaches and in the sea. Waste not only endangers marine life but contaminates natural water sources in a country where more than 95 percent of the population still uses water from wells and other natural sources. At the same time, rotting garbage produces the toxic greenhouse gas, methane, which has been known to contribute to climate change. Climate change will mean that Haiti will experience decreased average rainfall, increased average temperatures, increased intensity of tropical storms, and desertification.[306]

Urgent recycling initiatives must be undertaken in Haiti. Plastic and paper recycling facilities will not only preserve the environment but create well-needed jobs, from factory workers to garbage pickers. At the same time, garbage can be recycled into much-needed garbage receptacles and other useful items. Young people, with their energy, optimism, and creativity, are the best suited to lead these initiatives. School children from the youngest age should learn the importance of caring for the environment and should be involved in community cleanup. Garbage receptacles should be placed in schools to encourage proper garbage disposal and to sort for recycling.

Mentorship

Churches represent one of the strongest community-based institutions in Haiti. Any serious community development initiative should include this local asset.

> Religious leaders often provide the community with a visionary framework for the development of programs promoting greater social and economic justice...Religious institutions also bring a relevant understanding of and appreciation for the necessity of ritual in the life of the community. Ritual, a symbolic re-enactment of tradition, pulls the myriad strands of community life together and allows each member of the religious community to participate as a valued part of the body.[307]

While providing much-needed remittances, Haiti's high emigration rate is a significant "brain drain" which destroys the social fabric of the society. There are many children growing up without their father or without either parent. Add to this, Haiti's high rural-urban migration has left many youths adrift and disillusioned. Consequently, there has been a sharp increase in teenage pregnancy and youth delinquency.[308] The Church must step in to provide social and moral support to these young people through mentorship programs.

The Haitian Church is full of young people, both adherents and visitors. But many Church leaders have never received any formal training in youth ministry. The Church should be equipped to more effectively meet the needs of this significant demographic through dynamic programs that teach "the values of a Protestant work ethic"—"responsibility, punctuality, respect, hard work, discipline," honesty and integrity at school and at work;[309] the theology of work (the divine mandate to work and exercise dominion over creation); and, sexual education (puberty, peer pressure, sexually transmitted diseases (STDs), unplanned pregnancies). I strongly recommend *Reach for Life* (2004)[310] in Haitian Creole as a youth development resource NGOs can invest in for use in schools and churches.

In addition to year-long programs, summer camps would be an ideal setting to implement all five aspects of this youth development strategy while encouraging the participation of members of the Diaspora.

Having looked at some strategies foreign aid donors can utilize to spur Haiti's development, in the next two chapters, we will look at the part the Haitian Church should play in this endeavor.

CHAPTER 15: PERCEPTION AND PROPHECY

"Sa nou bay pòv se Bondye nou pretel"
(When you give to the poor, you lend God).
—God will repay you when you help the poor.

Haiti clearly demonstrates that foreign aid success requires more than money. This fact underscores the critical role the Christian leaders must play in Haiti's economic development: first, as a prophetic voice; second, as an agent of racial reconciliation; and finally, as an agent of worldview transformation. We will explore the first role in this chapter.

In order to understand the Church's prophetic role, we must first understand the power of the spoken word. As I reflected on the impact of perception on present and future actions and outcomes, this led me to examine the importance of words as expressions of these perceptions. What is it about declaring something, pronouncing a word, whether good or bad, over someone else or oneself? Is it just reverse psychology? Is it just a self-fulfilling prophecy? What really is a blessing or a curse, and what power do they have when pronounced over a person, place, or situation?

What Is a Blessing?

A *blessing* may be defined as "the invoking of God's favor upon a person."[311] It demonstrates the power of words as portents of future things. The theological significance of pronouncing a blessing has sadly been lost in large part in the Christian tradition. It has been retained, however, by the other Abrahamic religions, Judaism and Islam, where believers greet each other with blessings of peace.[312] Apart from the "benediction" given at the end of some church services, many Western Christians do not understand the power of a blessing. In the Bible, priests (Numbers 6.22-27) and parents (Genesis 27:4) were charged with the solemn responsibility to pronounce blessings over their children and the nation at large. This sacred privilege is now the duty of every Christian (Romans 12:14) and the Church as a whole (Hebrews 13:20-21).

In the Bible, a special blessing was like a tangible possession. Jacob fled empty-handed from his twin brother, Esau, with nothing but a blessing. While Esau lived in opulence with his father, Isaac, Jacob had nothing but a stone to rest his head. Yet Esau hated Jacob because he had the blessing (Genesis 27-28).

Sticks and Stones…

God declared that His words are like an emissary sent out by a master to accomplish a specific task: "It will not return to me empty, but will accomplish what I desire and achieve the purpose for which I sent it" (Isaiah 55:11). Jesus went further to say, "The words that I speak to you are spirit, and they are life" (John 6:63, NKJV). As God's image-bearers, humans have a measure of that same power in our words. Our words can either be a healing, life-giving fountain or a devouring wildfire kindled by hell itself (see

Proverbs 12:18; Proverbs 15:4; James 3:6). It all depends on the source of our inspiration.

The power and importance of words can also be seen in the names of Satan in the Bible. The name Satan itself means "accuser" or "slanderer" (Zechariah 3:1). This suggests that Satan's greatest weapons are words. It should not be taken for granted that the biggest spiritual attacks people face are psychological. Satan is also called the "father of lies" (John 8:44), who uses lies and half-truths to torment, accuse, distract, mislead, and in effect to, destroy people's lives and relationships by aborting the future God has for them. Satan does this by convincing them to leave the path God wants for them and to stay off it. This tactic demonstrates the power of words. It is not surprising that Jesus said, "You will know the truth, and the truth will set you free" (John 8:32). Living a lie is slavery.

While many people speculate about the Voodoo ceremony held before Haiti's battle of independence and wonder if this invoked a curse over the country, they are unaware that many Haitians and foreigners alike pronounce curses over Haiti every day without being aware of it. Researchers have found that verbalized perceptions, especially negative portrayals of place, affect everything from tourism to foreign direct investment and economic development overall.[313] Words can have destructive power, contrary to the rhyme we are taught as children: "Sticks and stones may break my bones, but words can never harm me."

Perceptions and Parenting

The power of words underscores the need for Haitian parents to be careful about what they say to their children about Haiti and its future. Wilkinson and Pickett (2009) give insights into how a parent's adversity, particularly socioeconomic inequality, can affect their children.

> When people talk of poor parenting, or say people lack parenting skills, the truth is often that the way parents treat their children actually serves to pass on their experience of adversity to the child. Although this is usually an unconscious process, in which the parent simply feels short-tempered, depressed, or at their wit's end, it is sometimes also conscious...Many studies have shown that forms of behaviour experienced in childhood tend to be mirrored in adulthood. Children who have, for example, experienced violence or abuse are more likely to become abusing and violent when they reach adulthood.[314]

What the authors describe above are not only coping mechanisms but also cycles of dysfunction. Conditioning children to expect nothing but adversity will spoil their outlook on life and influence them to behave in ways that may create the very adversity they were taught to expect. In this way, adversity can be perpetuated across generations; that is, it can become a generational curse. Haiti has experienced many years of adversity, but I encourage Haitians to balance the difficult realities with Haiti's resources and potential as they talk about the country. In this way, the next generation will not see Haiti as a sinking ship, doomed to fail. They will stay and rebuild Haiti.

Perceptions and Politics

The Church should be a prophetic voice for political change in Haiti. The widespread belief among evangelicals in Haiti is that politics is inherently corrupt and corrupting. As such, the Church's role is to pray and leave politics to corrupt officials. Very few Christians vote. They have a fatalistic view of the country. "Haitian politics will never change," they say. And by staying away from politics, this becomes a self-fulfilling prophecy.

The Church should also go beyond vision-casting to active involvement in representational politics. One of the controversial issues Maggay (2004) explores in her book, *Transforming Society*, is that of Christians' involvement in the political process, particularly expressing dissent. Many Christians use the Bible's command to respect political figures to mean that Christians should be pacifists. But Maggay insists that Scripture is "unclear and undogmatic" on the issue of political belief, limiting itself to "a description of what the state must do."[315] Because the government must be constantly re-evaluated and readjusted in order to remain effective in addressing the ever-changing needs and circumstances of its people, criticism and dissent are "not only desirable but imperative."[316] Based on 1 Peter 2:14, God institutes political leaders "to institute order, to

149

restrain evil and promote the good."[317] But when they fail to do so, "the Church must resist with the full force of her authority to speak a prophetic word."[318]

Prophetic Leadership

The Haitian Church has a divine mandate to change Haiti's narrative through prophecy. Haiti desperately needs prophetic leaders like the prophet Ezekiel to speak to the country's seemingly impossible situation. When asked by the Sovereign Lord if a vast number of dry bones could come back to life, even the prophet was hesitant and uncertain (Ezekiel 37:3). However, led by the Spirit of God, Ezekiel followed the Lord's command to:

> Prophesy to these bones and say to them, "Dry bones, hear the word of the Lord! This is what the Sovereign Lord says to these bones: I will make breath enter you, and you will come to life. I will attach tendons to you and make flesh come upon you and cover you with skin; I will put breath in you, and you will come to life. Then you will know that I am the Lord."
>
> Ezekiel 37:4-6

In his stirring work, *The Prophetic Imagination*, Brueggemann explains that "the task of prophetic ministry is to nurture, nourish, and evoke a consciousness and perception alternative to the consciousness and perception of the dominant culture around us."[319]

The prophet ushers in this alternative consciousness by keeping two elements in balance: "criticizing" and "energizing."[320] That means being fully cognizant of the present negative reality while being optimistic and motivational about a better future.

The Bible prophets "understood the distinctive power of language, the capacity to speak in ways that evoke newness 'fresh from the word.'"[321] The author's emphasis on a community being "rooted in energizing memories and summoned by radical hopes"[322] echoes two dominant themes of Appreciative Inquiry: Carrying forward the best parts of the past into the future and crafting "provocative propositions" which are "positive images phrased as if they were already happening."[323]

Haiti desperately needs prophetic leaders because its problems can seem intractable and overwhelming. Such situations require a spiritual "breakthrough," which may be considered the biblical counterpart to the leadership concept of transformational change. According to the Merriam-Webster Dictionary (2020), a *breakthrough* is "an act or instance of moving through or beyond an obstacle" or "a sudden advance."[324] When God was getting ready to deliver His people after seventy years of Babylonian captivity, He declared through the prophet Isaiah, "Do not remember the former things, Nor consider the things of old. Behold, I will do a new thing, Now it shall spring forth..." (Isaiah 43:18-19, NKJV).

In the next chapter, I will conclude by looking at the other two major roles the Church must assume in Haiti's transformation: an agent of racial reconciliation and worldview transformation.

CHAPTER 16: WORLDVIEW TRANSFORMATION

"Bay kou bliye, pote mak sonje" (If you hit me, I'll forget;
but if you wound me, I'll remember).
—Some offenses are unforgivable.

Racial Reconciliation

The Church is strategically positioned to help Haitians rethink their perceptions or beliefs about themselves, their country, foreigners, and God. This is the precursor to the second role the Haitian Church must play in the development of Haiti as a catalyst of racial reconciliation. Christians should take the helm in reconciliation between the different social classes within the country and between Haitians and foreigners. The Bible has a unique message of reconciliation between God and people and different people groups. "In Christ Jesus... There is neither Jew nor Gentile, neither slave nor free, nor is there male and female, for you are all one in Christ Jesus" (Galatians 3:26, 28). "For he himself is our peace, who has made the two groups one and has destroyed the barrier, the dividing wall of hostility" (Ephesians 2:14).

Many Haitians view foreigners with suspicion and distrust at best or animosity at worst. Others have a complex of inferiority that breeds an unhealthy dependency on *blan* (whites) to deliver them from their despair. Haiti's challenge is to not internalize the injustices committed against it, which would, in turn, create a victim mentality and a fatalistic outlook.[325] "We can easily define ourselves by our wounds, or even actually *become* our wounds, in which case we end up passing the wounds on to others—and back to ourselves," which leads to violence.[326] McNeil and Richardson (2009) concur: "Tragically, we always become what we hate. Hatred merely fuels a never-ending cycle of violence and revenge."[327] The Church of Jesus Christ is strategically positioned and divinely empowered to break this cycle of hurt, unforgiveness, and violence.

The path towards sustainable economic development, especially for small developing economies, includes tourism and foreign direct investment.[328] Both of these strategies involve partnerships with foreigners. Therefore Haitians, especially those who consider themselves Patriots, should beware of the dangers of reverse racism. Brazilian educator and philosopher, Paulo Freire, picks up on this theme when he insightfully wrote,

> Sooner or later, being less human leads the oppressed to struggle against those who made them so. In order for this struggle to have meaning, the oppressed must not, in seeking to regain their humanity ...become in turn oppressors of the oppressors, but rather restorers of the humanity of both.[329]

While history has shown that some foreign aid donors do have ulterior motives for giving aid, this is certainly not true of all. Many donors genuinely want to improve the lives of Haiti's poor, even though they may go about this in counterproductive ways. Negative experiences with foreigners in Haiti's past may also make some

Haitians suspicious of the motives foreigners have for working in Haiti. It is wrong to assume that all foreigners come to Haiti to exploit the country. In the same way that thousands of Haitians migrate each year to work overseas, foreigners can also visit or live in Haiti for legitimate work-related reasons. Therefore, I would encourage Haitians to reserve judgment and maintain a positive outlook when interacting with foreigners. Importantly, they should try not to poison their children's minds against foreigners nor portray Haitians as inferior to foreigners.

Worldview Transformation

Linthicum explains that "What a society *believes* will radically shape how that society chooses to order its corporate life and distribute its resources—not the other way around!"[330] Since "*religion* simply means 'that which fences about,'"[331] there must be a fundamental shift in what Haitians believe about God and other people and the moral laws that govern their relationships with them. This highlights the final role the Haitian Church needs to play in the transformation of Haitian society, namely, setting people free from spiritual bondage by preaching the Gospel and discipling believers. One's sociology is indelibly tied to one's theology.[332]

Demons of Poverty

There is a popular Haitian maxim that says that Haitians are 90 percent Catholics, 10 percent Protestants, and 100 percent

Voodooists.[333] This saying is an exaggeration, but it captures some of the reality of the prevalence of Voodoo in Haiti. The dominance of Voodoo in Haiti has far-reaching implications for the country's social and economic development.

Firstly, within its pantheon of gods are the *Petro lwas,* which "derive from the oppressive conditions of slavery and are associated with the Haitian revolution; they are said to inspire violence and are associated with the rage of slaves against their masters."[334] The violent political uprisings throughout Haiti's history that have crippled the country's economic development have been attributed to these gods. The Church must advocate for more constructive forms of dissent and political action.

Secondly, Voodoo keeps its adherents locked in economic poverty through its myriad sacrifices. At set times every year or if told to do so in a dream, Voodoo worshippers must make very costly sacrifices of chickens, goats, cows, various foods, expensive perfumes, and jewelry to their ancestral spirit or *lwa.* To disobey incurs the god's wrath bringing sickness or death.[335]

Finally, Haitian Voodoo is a religion of fear. Historically, political leaders have been known to use "Vodou as a key instrument for frightening the populace into accepting [their] rule."[336] Many Haitians are also afraid to succeed because of jealous family and friends who they fear will use magic to destroy them. A worldview dominated by fear is counterproductive to development.[337]

Spiritual Warfare

One common mistake many foreign aid workers in Haiti make is dismissing Voodoo as the empty superstitions of pre-modern people. Another tendency is for Christian missionaries to Haiti to ignore or downplay the existence of evil spirits and spiritual warfare. Others do not believe in witchcraft at all. Some, like Hiebert (2008), purport that magic "does not involve supplicating spirit beings in hope that they will respond."[338] He believes people get magic powers from abstract formulas. However, the Bible teaches otherwise:

> Let no one be found among you who sacrifices their son or daughter in the fire, who practices divination or sorcery, interprets omens, engages in witchcraft, or casts spells, or who is a medium or spiritist or who consults the dead. Anyone who does these things is detestable to the Lord...
>
> Deuteronomy 18:10-12a

Throughout the Old Testament, God denounced all forms of the occult. In the end, He handed over His people, Israel, to their enemies because of the detestable sacrifices they performed to win the favor of pagan gods who the Apostle Paul later revealed were actually demons (see 1 Corinthians 10:20).

Spiritual warfare is real, as demonstrated by the Gospels' vivid accounts of Jesus' confrontation and domination of evil spirits. Furthermore, Christians in the early Church understood that demonic attacks did not cease once one became a Christian. They were taught explicitly that "Our struggle is not against flesh and blood, but against the rulers, against the authorities, against the powers of this dark world and against the spiritual forces of evil in the heavenly realms" (Ephesians 6:12).

Many Haitians also misunderstand Voodoo. One common mistake is confusing Voodoo with Haitian culture. Therefore, they think that since they are Haitian, they are automatically Voodooists in one way or another. While religion in general is considered part of a people's culture, the Bible teaches that our relationship with God is a matter of personal faith. Serving the God of the Bible demands exclusivity. Following Christ is not a group decision but an individual one.

Other Haitians feel that Western colonization has stolen so much of their cultural identity and pride and that Voodoo is all they have left. For them, practicing Voodoo is being Afrocentric: honoring their roots, their heritage, and their ancestors. However, there are many other distinctive aspects of Haitian culture that a Haitian can use to celebrate their heritage that do not involve the worship of ancestral spirits and do not violate their Christian faith.

Weh Unnu Nuh Leffi People Dem Alone?

I remember preparing for my first international mission trip to Kenya as a bright-eyed, bushy-tailed nineteen-year-old ready to take on the world. When I told my non-religious dentist about my trip, he was not impressed. He retorted in fine Jamaican parlance, "Weh unnu nuh leffi people dem alone?" In other words, "Why don't you leave the people alone? Why do you want to overrun their rich indigenous culture with Westernization?" But seasoned community development practitioners like Dr. Melba Maggay from the Philippines know that for development efforts to be effective, we must "wrestle with the strongholds of the mind"[339] before, during, and after implementing any development strategy. Worldview transformation plays "a central role in poverty-alleviation efforts. In fact, in some cases, people's worldviews are so distorted that it is difficult to bring about any progress at all until the people undergo a major paradigm shift."[340] Therefore, NGOs must make training Haitian Christian leaders a priority so they can take the helm in worldview transformation.

In their book, *Demons of Poverty*, Boers and Stoner cite a study conducted by Lawrence Harrison, a secular anthropologist, which found that

> Animist religions... in which what happens in life is determined by a pantheon of capricious spirits, presents an extreme case of progress-resistant culture, as we have seen in Haitian Voodoo.[341]

Boers and Stoner conclude that "one of the most significant influences behind Haitian poverty [is] a nation-wide commitment to a religion of fear, futility and fatalism."[342] Harrison recommends that "what countries like Haiti need, is to encourage conversion of those practicing animist religions to more progress-prone religions" like Christianity.[343] As the Bible makes clear, people can never truly change until they change their minds (see Romans 12:2).

CARRY ON

"Men anpil chay pa lou" (Many hands make the load light).

The story is told of how, as England prepared to face Germany's formidable forces in 1939, "the British government commissioned a series of posters" to put all over England.[344] The objective was to boost the morale and inspire the confidence of its citizens and troops. The posters had encouraging slogans that were clear and simply presented. The first poster stated the following.

YOUR COURAGE
YOUR CHEERFULNESS
YOUR RESOLUTION
WILL BRING US VICTORY

Soon afterward, a second poster urged the following.

FREEDOM IS IN PERIL
DEFEND IT WITH ALL YOUR MIGHT

More than 2.5 million copies of a third poster were printed in case Britain faced severe setbacks during the war. But they were never released to the public. Sixty years later, a bookstore owner discovered a copy that read:

KEEP CALM
AND CARRY ON

Haiti's journey to economic prosperity will be challenging. There will be numerous setbacks. To those committed to this adventure, it is important to "Keep calm and carry on." Some may perceive that Haiti's woes are "beyond the reach of any mortals currently on the scene."[345] However, others are optimistic about Haiti's future, as am I, based on Isaiah 61.4, which describes the exploits of those who are transformed by Messiah:

> *"They will rebuild the ancient ruins*
> *and restore the places long devastated;*
> *they will renew the ruined cities*
> *that have been devastated for generations."*

APPENDICES

Appendix 1: COVID Death Rate for Selected Caribbean Countries

Country	Population[4]	COVID Deaths[5] (As of Nov. 15, 2021)	COVID death rate/ 100,000 citizens
Cuba	11,326,616	8,282	73.11
Panama	4,314,767	7,342	170.15
Uruguay	3,473,730	6,101	175.63
Dominican Republic	10,847,910	4,170	38.44
Jamaica	2,961,167	2,327	78.58
Trinidad and Tobago	1,399,488	1,858	132.76
Haiti	11,402,528	708	6.2
Bahamas	393,244	665	169.1

---

[4] Retrieved from https://www.worldometers.info/population/countries-in-lat-in-america-and-the-caribbean-by-population/

[5] Retrieved from https://www.statista.com/statistics/1103965/latin-america-ca-ribbean-coronavirus-deaths/

Appendix 2: Q Set

A. Statements about foreign aid

1. Foreign aid helps reduce problems in Haiti.
2. Vaccines from NGOs are good.
3. I am grateful for healthcare from NGOs.
4. NGOs have good schools.
5. NGOs have projects that create lasting change.

B. Statements about foreign aid donors

6. Aid donors are honest.
7. Foreign aid donors live here because the cost of living is less than in their country.
8. I am uncomfortable when foreigners take photos of me or the country.
9. Foreign aid donors work in Haiti to raise money for themselves.
10. Many foreigners are spies.
11. Foreigners come to exploit the country's resources.
12. Foreigners respect Haitians.
13. Aid donors build schools and orphanages because they love Haitian children.
14. Foreign countries want to control Haiti.
15. Aid donors help because they feel sorry for Haitians.
16. Haitians and foreigners can be friends.
17. NGOs work to give Haitians a better life.
18. Foreigners bring a lot of new diseases to Haiti.
19. Foreign NGOs use Haitians as guinea pigs for medical research.
20. Most of the money raised for Haiti stays overseas because foreigners get the jobs.
21. NGOs help me a lot.
22. People working for NGOs are only concerned about keeping their jobs.

C. Statements about how Haitians perceive themselves

    a. General statements

23. Haitians use magic to prevent others from "stealing" their White sponsor.
24. Haitian politicians lie about disasters in Haiti in order to get more foreign aid.
25. Haitian politicians do not develop the country in order to get more foreign aid.
26. Haitian food is better than imported food.
27. Haitians have more confidence in foreigners than in themselves.
28. Haiti is beautiful.
29. Haiti has a lot of natural resources.
30. There is hope for Haiti.

    b. What Haitians think about themselves (Self-efficacy)

31. Haiti will always need foreign aid.
32. I am proud that Haiti was the first Black republic in the world.
33. Haiti is the worst country in the world.
34. People must go overseas to get a good job.
35. Out of politeness, I will go along with a foreigner's idea or project even if I don't think it's good.
36. Only foreigners can fix Haiti's problems.
37. Haitians are as intelligent as foreigners.
38. Haiti is poor because Haitians are selfish.
39. I won't live in any other country besides Haiti.
40. Magic is the only thing Haitians are good at.

    c. What Haitians think about work (Work ethic)

41. There are jobs some Haitians wouldn't do in Haiti, but they do overseas.

42. Some Haitians would rather be unemployed than do menial jobs.
43. Many Haitians don't work because they get money from overseas.
44. Many Haitians don't save because they get money from overseas.
45. I don't like to work for someone else because that is like slavery.
46. Many Haitians think only office work is respectable work.
47. Many Haitians choose to spend all their time praying instead of working.
48. "Work is freedom."
49. Many Haitians believe going to school is a waste of time.
50. You can succeed in Haiti if you work hard.

Appendix 3: Score Sheet

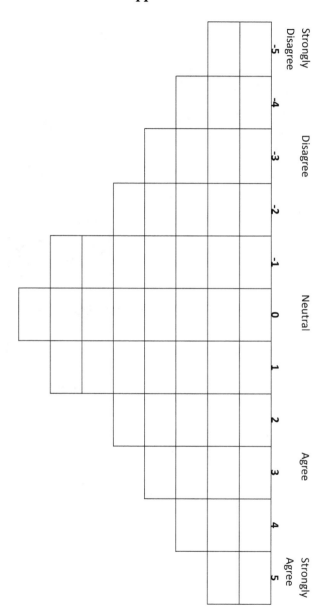

Appendix 4: A Completed Game Board

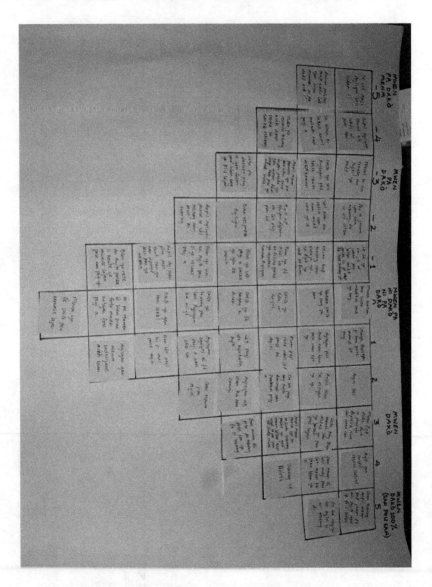

NOTES

[1] Chaparro, L., "Two Sisters Flipped a Coin, One of Them Was Sent to Hell," *Daily Beast,* September 22, 2021, https://www.thedailybeast.com/two-sisters-flipped-a-coin-in-del-rio-one-of-them-was-sent-to-hell

[2] Kristoff, M. and Panarelli, L. (2010). Haiti: A Republic of NGOs? https://www.usip.org/sites/default/files/PB%2023%20Haiti%20a%20Republic%20of%20NGOs.pdf; See also Steinke, A. (2020). Haiti ten years after douz Janvye: Humanitarian perspectives and lessons learned from the 2010 earthquake in Haiti. https://www.chaberlin.org/publications/haiti-ten-years-after-douz-janvye/

[3] Labrador, R. and Roy, D., "Haiti's Troubled Path to Development," *Council on Foreign Relations*, September 17, 2021, https://www.cfr.org/backgrounder/haitis-troubled-path-development

[4] USDS. (2009). Founding of Liberia, 1847. https://2001-2009.state.gov/r/pa/ho/time/dwe/16337.htm

[5] The World Bank. (2015). Haiti: Towards a new narrative. https://documents.worldbank.org/en/publication/documents-reports/documentdetail/319651467986293030/haiti-towards-a-new-narrative-systematic-country-diagnostic

[6] Thomas, R. (2014). *Roots of Haiti's Vodou-Christian faith: African and Catholic origins.* Santa Barbara, CA: ABC-CLIO, p. 22

[7] The World Bank, 2015

[8] Thomas, 2014

[9] Encyclopedia.com. "Quisqueya," https://www.encyclopedia.com/humanities/encyclopedias-almanacs-transcripts-and-maps/quisqueya

[10] Desmangles, L. (1992). *The faces of the gods: Voodoo and Roman Catholicism in Haiti*. Chapel Hill, NC: University of North Carolina Press, p. 19

[11] USDS, 2009; See also BBC. (2019). Haiti country profile. https://www.bbc.com/news/world-latin-america-19548810#:~:text=Haiti%20became%20the%20world's%20first,in%20the%20early%2019th%20century

[12] L'Institut de Sauvegarde du Patrimoine National (ISPAN). (2020). "Haiti: The first Black republic and its monuments to freedom." Cap-Haitian, Haiti: Smithsonian Institution Traveling Exhibition Service (SITES).

[13] Institut Haïtien de Statistique et d'Informatique (IHSI). (2015). Population Totale, Population De 18 Ans Et Plus. https://web.archive.org/web/20151106110552/http://www.ihsi.ht/pdf/projection/Estimat_PopTotal_18ans_Menag2015.pdf

[14] CountryMeters. (2019). Haiti population. https://countrymeters.info/en/Haiti

[15] MapsOpenSource. Haiti Map Black and White. http://mapsopensource.com/haiti-map-black-and-white.html

[16] Central Intelligence Agency [CIA]. (2019). The world factbook: Haiti. https://www.cia.gov/library/publications/the-world-factbook/geos/ha.html ; See also Caribbean Journal (2020). Ranking the Caribbean by population age. https://www.caribjournal.com/2013/11/04/ranking-the-caribbean-by-population-age/#:~:text=So%20what's%20the%20country%20in,ages%20of%200%20and%2014., 2020

[17] Thomas, 2014, p. 25

[18] CIA, 2019

[19] Adelman, C. (2011). Haiti: Testing the limits of government aid and

philanthropy. https://www.jstor.org/stable/24590799

[20] The World Bank, 2015

[21] The World Bank, 2015, p. 44

[22] The World Bank, 2015

[23] The World Bank, 2015, p.15

[24] Labrador, R. and Roy, D., "Haiti's Troubled Path to Development."

[25] The World Bank, 2015, p. 16

[26] The World Bank, 2015, p. 33

[27] Hedges, B., Cohen, W., Timyan, J., and Yang, Z. (2018). Haiti's biodiversity threatened by nearly complete loss of primary forest. https://doi.org/10.1073/pnas.1809753115

[28] Desmangles, 1992, p. 51

[29] The World Bank, 2015, p. xi

[30] The World Bank, 2015, p. 15

[31] The World Bank, 2015, p. 14

[32] Ramachandran, V. and Walz, J. (2015). Haiti: Where has all the money gone? https://www.jstor.org/stable/24573148, p. 27

[33] Charles, J.and Fils-aimé, J., "Haiti President Jovenel Moïse assassinated in middle-of-the-night attack at his home," *Miami Herald*, July 7, 2021, https://www.miamiherald.com/article252616688.html

[34] Domonoske, C., "14 Months After Elections Began, Haiti Finally Has a President-Elect," *National Public Radio* (NPR), January 4, 2017, https://www.npr.org/sections/thetwo-way/2017/01/04/508171191/14-months-after-elections-began-haiti-finally-has-a-president-elect

[35] Lemaire, S., "Haiti President's Term Will End in 2022, Biden Administration Says," *Voice of America*, (VOA), February, 5, 2021, https://www.voanews.com/

americas/haiti-presidents-term-will-end-2022-biden-administration-says

[36] The World Bank, 2015, p. 33

[37] Hiebert, P. G. (2008). *Transforming worldviews: An anthropological understanding of how people change.* Grand Rapids, MI: Baker Academic, p. 15

[38] Hiebert, 2008, p. 69

[39] Thomas, 2014

[40] Desmangles, p. 10

[41] Hiebert, 2008, p. 118

[42] Steyne, P. M. (1996). *Gods of power: A study of the beliefs and practices of animists.*
Columbia, SC: Impact International Foundation, p. 34

[43] Thomas, 2014, p. 87

[44] Edmonds, B. and Gonzalez, M. (2010). *Caribbean religious history: An introduction.* New York, NY: New York University Press, p.109

[45] Van Rheenen, G. (1991). *Communicating Christ in animistic contexts.*
Grand Rapids, MI:
Baker Book House, p. 20

[46] Thomas, 2014, p. 203

[47] Thomas, 2014

[48] Hiebert, 2008, p. 118

[49] Wilde, J., "The Occult is Having a Moment," *Morning Brew*, October 29, 2021, https://www.morningbrew.com/daily/stories/2021/10/29/the-occult-is-having-a-moment

[50] Wiles, K., "Witchcraft goes mainstream, and becomes big business," *Marketplace*, February 14, 2020, https://www.marketplace.org/2020/02/14/

witchcraft-goes-mainstream-becomes-big-business/

[51] James, E. (2012). Witchcraft, bureaucraft, and the social life of (US)aid in Haiti. *Cultural Anthropology*, 27(1), 50–75. https://www.jstor.org/stable/41336318, p. 50

[52] James, 2012, p. 51

[53] James, 2012, pp. 50–51

[54] Comaroff, J. and Comaroff J. L. (1999). Occult Economies and the Violence of Abstraction: Notes from the South African Postcolony. *American Ethnologist*, 26(2), 279-303., p. 282

[55] James, E. (2010). *Democratic insecurities: Violence, trauma, and intervention in Haiti*. Berkeley, CA: University of California Press.

[56] James, 2012, p. 51

[57] James, 2012, p. 52

[58] James, 2012, p. 62

[59] James, 2012, p. 53

[60] Wilde, J., "The Occult is Having a Moment."

[61] Wiles, K., "Witchcraft goes mainstream, and becomes big business."

[62] Wiles, K., "Witchcraft goes mainstream, and becomes big business."

[63] Ledbetter, C., "Meghan Markle Just Wore a Bracelet Designed To 'Ward Off Undesired Energy'," *The Huffington Post,* November 9, 2021, https://www.yahoo.com/news/meghan-markle-just-wore-bracelet-223431133.html

[64] Hiebert, 2008, p. 129

[65] Hiebert, 2008, p. 130

[66] Hossain, N. (2004). The difficult relationship between aid donors and recipients: Findings from post-aid dependent Bangladesh. https://assets.publishing.service.gov.uk/media/57a08cd1e5274a27b200144d/

R8248appendix1.pdf, p. 11

[67] Hossain, 2004

[68] Hossain, 2004

[69] Hossain, 2004, p. 13

[70] Hossain, 2004, p. 21

[71] De Beer, N., "Caribbean pearl's descent to disaster," *Independent Online*, October 3, 2019, https://www.iol.co.za/business-report/opinion/caribbean-pearls-descent-to-disaster-33944272

[72] Desmangles, 1992, pp. 20-21

[73] Thomas, 2014; See also Kristof, N. D. and WuDunn, S. (2009). *Half the sky: Turning oppression into opportunity for women worldwide*. New York: Knopf Doubleday Publishing Group (Kindle 5).

[74] Desmangles, 1992; Thomas, 2014

[75] Thomas, 2014

[76] Thomas, 2014

[77] Gisler cited in Desmangles, 1992, p. 24

[78] Heinl cited in Thomas, 2014, p. 19

[79] Thomas, 2014, p. 20

[80] Desmangles, 1992, p. 29

[81] Thomson, H., "Study of Holocaust survivors finds trauma passed on to children's genes," *The Guardian,* August 21, 2015, https://www.theguardian.com/science/2015/aug/21/study-of-holocaust-survivors-finds-trauma-passed-on-to-childrens-genes, para. 4

[82] Thomas, 2014

[83] Desmangles, 1992, p. 29

[84] Logan, R. (1961). The US "colonial experiment" in Haiti, https://www.jstor.

org/stable/40394102, p. 437

85 Daut, M., "When France extorted Haiti—the greatest heist in history," *The Conversation*, June 30, 2020, https://theconversation.com/when-france-extorted-haiti-the-greatest-heist-in-history-137949

86 Daut, 2020

87 Labrador, R. and Roy, D., "Haiti's Troubled Path to Development."

88 Daut, 2020

89 Daut, 2020, para. 1

90 Desmangles, 1992, p. 40

91 Britannica (2020). The Haitian Revolution. https://www.britannica.com/place/Haiti/The-Haitian-Revolution

92 Sperling, D., "In 1825, Haiti paid France $21 billion to preserve its independence—time for France to pay it back," *Forbes,* December 6, 2017, https://www.forbes.com/sites/realspin/2017/12/06/in-1825-haiti-gained-independence-from-france-for-21-billion-its-time-for-france-to-pay-it-back/#34d5ed80312b

93 Desmangles, 1992, p. 39

94 Burney, S. (2012). Edward Said and postcolonial theory: Disjunctured identities and the subaltern voice. https://www.jstor.org/stable/42981699, p. 53

95 Burney, 2012, p. 50

96 Desmangles, 1992

97 US Department of State Archives. (2001-2009). U.S. Invasion and Occupation of Haiti, 1915–34. https://2001-2009.state.gov/r/pa/ho/time/wwi/88275.htm, para. 2.

98 US Department of State Archives (2001-2009), para. 4

[99] Desmangles, 1992, pp. 48

[100] US Department of State Archives, 2001-2009, para. 5

[101] US Department of State Archives, 2001-2009, para. 5

[102] Potter, A. (2009). Voodoo, zombies, and mermaids: US newspaper coverage of Haiti. https://www.jstor.org/stable/40377381, p. 216

[103] Thomas, 2014, p. 23

[104] Thomas, 2014, p. 23

[105] Thomas, 2014, p. 23

[106] Britannica. (2020). Military regimes and the Duvaliers. https://www.britannica.com/place/Haiti/Military-regimes-and-the-Duvaliers

[107] Hossain, 2004

[108] Thomas, 2014, p. 23

[109] Desmangles, 1992

[110] History of Haiti cited in Thomas, 2014, p. 23

[111] Ramachandran and Walz, 2015

[112] Daut, 2020

[113] Ramachandran and Walz, 2015

[114] Ramachandran and Walz, 2015, p. 28

[115] Ramachandran and Walz, 2015, p. 28

[116] Ramachandran and Walz, 2015

[117] The World Bank, 2015

[118] The World Bank, 2015, p. 7

[119] Ridgeway, J. (Ed.) (1994). Untitled introduction to the section on The Coup and US Foreign Policy. *The Haiti files: Decoding the crisis.* (Washington, D.C.: Essential Books.), p. 85

[120] Ridgeway, 1994

[121] The World Bank, 2015

[122] Trading Economics. (2020). Haiti—GINI index. https://tradingeconomics.com/haiti/gini-index-wb-data.html

[123] Jadotte, E. (2008). The state and structure of inequality in the Republic of Haiti. https://dialnet.unirioja.es/descarga/articulo/3137590.pdf

[124] Schuller, M. (2009). Gluing globalization: NGOs as intermediaries in Haiti. https://www.jstor.org/stable/24497527

[125] Schuller, 2009, p. 94

[126] Slideshare. (2017). The Haitian elite- the richest Haitians. https://www.slideshare.net/haitieconomie/la-bourgeoisie-hatienne-les-riches-hatiens-the-hatian-elite-the-richest-hatians

[127] Desmangles, 1992

[128] Jadotte, 2008, p. 21

[129] Jadotte, 2008, p. 23

[130] Ramachandran and Walz, 2015, p. 26

[131] Garland, C. (2015). The visual rhetoric of 'voluntourists' and aid workers in post-earthquake Haiti. http://www.jstor.com/stable/44734832

[132] Garland, 2015, p. 86

[133] Garland, 2015, p. 82

[134] Wilkinson, R. and Pickett, K. (2009). *The spirit level: Why greater equality makes societies stronger.* (New York, NY: Bloomsbury Press.), p. 113

[135] Potter, 2009, p. 208

[136] Potter, 2009, p. 210

[137] Potter, 2009, p. 209

[138] Garland, 2015, p. 84

[139] Coupeau cited in Garland, 2015, p. 84

[140] Garland, 2015, p. 84

[141] Potter, 2009, p. 217

[142] Potter, 2009, p. 224

[143] Pierre-Pierre cited in Potter, 2009, p. 211

[144] Schwartz, T. (2017). *The great Haiti humanitarian aid swindle.* (Scotts Valley, CA: CreateSpace.), p. 48

[145] Schwartz, T., "Haiti's Questionable Earthquake Death Toll," *Haiti Liberté,* January 16, 2019, https://haitiliberte.com/haitis-questionable-earthquake-death-toll/

[146] Thornton, C. and Dupain, E., "Haiti faces hunger as Covid-19 looms," *CNN,* May 8, 2020, https://edition.cnn.com/2020/05/08/americas/haiti-famine-coronavirus-intl/index.html, para. 2

[147] TV5monde, "Coronavirus en Haïti : Famine et crise sanitaire inquiètent,"*TV5monde,* May 6, 2020, https://information.tv5monde.com/info/coronavirus-en-haiti-famine-et-crise-sanitaire-inquietent-358198

[148] Regan, J., "Behind the Covid numbers in Haiti," *The North American Congress on Latin America,* June 9, 2020, https://nacla.org/news/2020/06/09/behind-covid-numbers-haiti, para. 1

[149] Regan, J., "Behind the Covid numbers in Haiti."

[150] Regan, J., "Behind the Covid numbers in Haiti."

[151] Paultre, A., "Haiti receives more deportees from U.S. despite coronavirus fears," *Reuters*, April 23, 2020, https://www.reuters.com/article/us-health-coronavirus-haiti-deportation-idUSKCN22606Y

[152] Charles, J., "Why Has COVID Claimed Few Lives in Haiti Despite Lax Rules?" *Miami Herald,* December 16, 2020, https://www.govtech.com/em/safety/why-does-covid-19-claim-so-few-lives-in-haiti-despite-lax-rules.html

[153] Charles, J., "Why Has COVID Claimed Few Lives in Haiti Despite Lax Rules?"

[154] Beaubien, J., "One of the world's poorest countries has one of the world's lowest COVID death rates," *National Public Radio*, May 4, 2021, https://www.npr.org/sections/goatsandsoda/2021/05/04/992544022/one-of-the-worlds-poorest-countries-has-one-of-the-worlds-lowest-covid-death-rat, para. 1

[155] CDC. (2021). COVID-19 in Haiti. https://wwwnc.cdc.gov/travel/notices/covid-4/coronavirus-haiti

[156] OSAC. (2019). Haiti 2019 crime and safety report. https://www.osac.gov/Content/Report/b038d0a0-cc5a-4427-a753-15f4aebea7a9

[157] Worldometer. (2020). Haiti population (2020). https://www.worldometers.info/world-population/haiti-population/

[158] Haiti Libre, "Haiti-UN: 42% increase in homicides in Haiti (2019)," *Haiti Libre,* February 20, 2020, https://www.haitilibre.com/en/news-30075-haiti-un-42-increase-in-homicides-in-haiti-2019.html

[159] Fieldstadt, E., "Murder map: Deadliest U.S. cities," *CBS News,* April 19, 2021, https://www.cbsnews.com/pictures/murder-map-deadliest-u-s-cities/58/

[160] Hart, R., "Fourth Of July Weekend Saw Highest Number Of Mass Shootings Than Any Other Weekend In 2021," *Forbes,* July 6, 2021, https://www.forbes.com/sites/roberthart/2021/07/06/fourth-of-july-weekend-saw-highest-number-of-mass-shootings-than-any-other-weekend-in-2021/?sh=377f5ef4350d, para. 3

[161] Tucker, E., Jimenez, O., and Sgueglia, K., "More than 230 people fatally shot in shootings over the Fourth of July weekend," *CNN*, July 7, 2021, https://edition.cnn.com/2021/07/05/us/us-shootings-july-fourth-weekend/index.html

[162] Southall, A., "Cuomo Declares a Gun Violence Emergency in New York State," *The New York Times*, July 6, 2021, https://www.nytimes.com/2021/07/06/

nyregion/new-york-gun-violence-emergency.html

163 Statistica. (2020). Homicide in Latin America and the Caribbean—Statistics and facts. https://www.statista.com/topics/5388/homicide-in-latin-america-and-caribbean/

164 Statistica. (2020). Number of homicide victims in the Dominican Republic from 2014 to 2020, https://www.statista.com/statistics/312508/number-of-homicides-in-the-dominican-republic/

165 Statistica. (2020). Number of victims of intentional homicide in Haiti from 2010 to 2018. https://www.statista.com/statistics/312477/number-of-homicides-in-haiti/

166 Statistica. (2020). Homicide in Latin America and the Caribbean—Statistics and facts. https://www.statista.com/topics/5388/homicide-in-latin-america-and-caribbean/, para. 4

167 Statistica. (2020). Homicide rates in selected Latin American and Caribbean countries in 2020, https://www.statista.com/statistics/947781/homicide-rates-latin-america-caribbean-country/

168 USDS. (2021). Haiti Travel Advisory, https://travel.state.gov/content/travel/en/traveladvisories/traveladvisories/haiti-travel-advisory.html

169 Sanon, E. and Coto, D, "Surge in violence rattles Haiti as poverty, fear deepens," *Associated Press*, April 16, 2021, https://abcnews.go.com/International/wireStory/surge-violence-rattles-haiti-poverty-fear-deepens-77115520, para. 11

170 World Population Review. (2021). Human Trafficking Statistics by State 2021, https://worldpopulationreview.com/state-rankings/human-trafficking-statistics-by-state

171 https://worldpopulationreview.com/state-rankings/human-trafficking-

statistics-by-state

[172] World Population Review, 2021, para. 6

[173] World Population Review, 2021

[174] Ault, R. and Rodger, J., "Number of kidnappings in Birmingham is soaring and there are three main types," *Birmingham Mail*, November 25, 2020, https://www.birminghammail.co.uk/news/midlands-news/number-kidnappings-birmingham-soaring-three-19339077

[175] Hesson, T., "Nearly 3,300 migrants stranded in Mexico were kidnapped, raped or assaulted – report," *Reuters,* June 22, 2021, https://www.reuters.com/world/americas/nearly-3300-migrants-stranded-mexico-were-kidnapped-raped-or-assaulted-report-2021-06-22/

[176] Marsh, S., "'Descent into hell': Kidnapping explosion terrorizes Haiti," *Reuters*, April 26, 2021, https://www.reuters.com/world/americas/descent-into-hell-kidnapping-explosion-terrorizes-haiti-2021-04-26/

[177] Potter, 2006, p. 216

[178] Alexander, M. (2011). *The new Jim Crow: Mass incarceration in the age of colorblindness.* (New York: The New Press), p. 24

[179] Potter, 2009, p. 226

[180] Garland, 2015, p. 93

[181] Alexander, 2011, p. 5

[182] Dubois, L. (2012). *Haiti: The aftershocks of history.* New York: Metropolitan Books., p. 3

[183] Sperling, D., "In 1825, Haiti paid France $21 billion to preserve its independence -- time for France to pay it back," para. 2.

[184] HG.Org Legal Resources, What is the Difference Between Abduction and Kidnapping? https://www.hg.org/legal-articles/what-is-the-difference-between-

abduction-and-kidnapping-40587

[185] HG.Org Legal Resources, What is the Difference Between Abduction and Kidnapping?

[186] Farmer, P. (2006). *The Uses of Haiti*. Monroe, Maine: Common Courage Press. pp. 191–192

[187] Martínez-Zarzoso, I., Nowak-Lehmann, F., and Klasen, S. (2010). The economic benefits of giving aid in terms of donors' exports. https://ideas.repec.org/p/zbw/gdec10/28.html, p. 7

[188] Malik, K., "As a system, foreign aid is a fraud and does nothing for inequality," *The Guardian*, September 2, 2018, https://www.theguardian.com/commentisfree/2018/sep/02/as-a-system-foreign-aid-is-a-fraud-and-does-nothing-for-inequality

[189] Lundsgaarde, E., Breunig, C., and Prakash, A. (2010). Instrumental philanthropy: Trade and the allocation of foreign aid. https://www.jstor.org/stable/40983516

[190] Martínez-Zarzoso, et al., 2010

[191] Martínez-Zarzoso, et al., 2010, p. 2.

[192] Malik, 2018, para. 7

[193] Malik, 2018, para. 7

[194] McKinley, R. D., and Little, R., (1979). The US aid relationship: A test of the recipient need and the donor interest models. https://onlinelibrary.wiley.com/doi/abs/10.1111/j.1467-9248.1979.tb01201.x

[195] Faaland cited in Hossain, 2004, p. 8

[196] Hossain, 2004, p. 2

[197] Fisher, J., Nadler, A. and Whitcher-Alagna, S. (1982). Recipient reactions to aid. Retrieved from https://www.researchgate.net/

publication/232546326_Recipient_Reactions_to_Aid

[198] Ramachandran and Walz, 2015

[199] Ramachandran and Walz, 2015, pp. 29-30

[200] Ramachandran and Walz, 2015

[201] Ramachandran and Walz, 2015

[202] Fatton quoted in Berman, J., "How the wealthy use debt 'as a tool to screw the government and everybody else'," *Market Watch,* July 16, 2021, https://www.marketwatch.com/story/extra-credit-how-debt-can-mean-a-tax-advantage-for-some-and-jail-time-for-others-11626383631?siteid=yhoof2andyptr=yahoo, para. 29

[203] Doyle, M., "US urged to stop Haiti rice subsidies," *BBC News*, October 5, 2010, https://www.bbc.com/news/world-latin-america-11472874; See also Klarreich, K. and Polman, L., "The NGO Republic of Haiti," *The Nation*, November 19, 2012, https://www.thenation.com/article/archive/ngo-republic-haiti/

[204] Doyle, 2010; Klarreich and Polman, 2012

[205] Doyle, 2010, para. 12; See also PRI, "Oxfam: American food aid hurting Haiti," *The World*, October 6, 2010, https://theworld.org/stories/2010-10-06/oxfam-american-food-aid-hurting-haiti

[206] PRI, "Oxfam: American food aid hurting Haiti," para. 1

[207] Doyle, 2010

[208] Doyle, 2010, para. 2

[209] Doyle, 2010, para. 2–3

[210] Doyle, 2010; Klarreich and Polman, 2012

[211] Dobransky, S. (2015). The paradox of United States food aid and the challenge to realist theory. https://www.jstor.org/stable/24543835

CLAUDIA CHARLOT

[212] Dobransky, 2015, p. 64

[213] Dobransky, 2015, p. 65

[214] Dobransky, 2015, p. 87

[215] Meds and Food for Kids. (2021). Our Story. https://www.mfkhaiti.org/about

[216] Ramachandran and Walz, 2015

[217] Labrador, R., and Roy, D., "Haiti's Troubled Path to Development."

[218] Ramachandran and Walz, 2015, p. 32

[219] Ramachandran and Walz, 2015

[220] Ramachandran and Walz, 2015, p. 33; italics in the original

[221] Klarreich and Polman, 2012, para. 11

[222] Ramachandran and Walz, 2015, p. 33

[223] Ramachandran and Walz, 2015, p. 36

[224] Zanotti, L. (2010). Cacophonies of aid, failed state building and NGOs in Haiti: Setting the stage for disaster, envisioning the future. https://www.jstor.org/stable/27896575, p. 756

[225] Martínez-Zarzoso, et al., 2010

[226] Keck, M. (2015). Comparing the determinants of US-funded NGO aid versus US official development aid. https://www.jstor.org/stable/43654656, p. 1319

[227] Ahmed, S., and Potter, D. (2006). *NGOs in international politics.* Bloomfield: CT: Kumarian.

[228] Keck, 2015, p. 1328

[229] Klarreich and Polman, 2012

[230] Ramachandran and Walz, 2015

[231] Steinke, 2020, p. 4

[232] Ramachandran and Walz, 2015, p. 41

[233] Ramachandran and Walz, 2015, p. 43

184

234 Guha-Sapir, et al. cited in Ramachandran and Walz, 2015, p. 43

235 Ramachandran and Walz, 2015, p. 45

236 Freire, P. (2000). *Pedagogy of the Oppressed*. New York: Continuum., p. 44

237 Schwartz, 2017

238 Ramachandran and Walz, 2015

239 Holley, P., "The Red Cross had $500 million in Haitian relief money, but it built just 6 houses," *Washington Post*, June 4, 2015, https://www.washingtonpost.com/news/morning-mix/wp/2015/06/04/the-red-cross-had-500-million-in-haitian-relief-money-and-it-built-just-6-houses/

240 ProPublica cited in Holley, 2015, para. 9

241 Steinke, 2020, p. 4

242 Kpanake, L., Jean-Jacques, R., Sorum, P., Mullet, E. (2017). Haitian people's expectations regarding post-disaster humanitarian aid teams' actions. https://onlinelibrary.wiley.com/doi/abs/10.1111/dewb.12158, p. 3

243 Hossain, 2004; Kpanake, et al., 2017

244 Klarreich and Polman (2012) para. 7

245 Klarreich and Polman, 2012, para. 37

246 Ramachandran and Walz, 2015, p. 46

247 Morisseau-Leroy cited in Garland, 2015, pp. 79-80

248 Garland, 2015, p. 81

249 Garland, 2015, p. 89

250 Van Hoving, D., Wallis, L., Docrat, F., and De Vries, S. (2010). Haiti disaster tourism—A medical shame. https://doi.org/10.1017/S1049023X00008001, p. 202

251 Van Hoving, et al., (2010), p. 202

252 Sobhan, R. (2003). Globalization and the challenge to democracy. https://

www.researchgate.net/publication/239606030_Globalization_and_the_
challenge_to_democracy, p. 2

[253] Fisher, et al., 1982; See also Popkin, S. (1990). Welfare: Views from
the bottom. https://www.jstor.org/stable/800795; Pavetti, L., Holcolmb, P.,
and Duke, A. (1995). *Increasing participation in work and work-related
activities: Lessons from five state demonstration projects.* Washington, DC:
Urban Institute.; Hilhorst, D., Weijers, L., and Van Wessel, M. (2012). Aid
relations and aid legitimacy: Mutual imaging of aid workers and recipients
in Nepal. https://www.jstor.org/stable/41698796

[254] Viard, R., "Haiti's role in the independence of Latin American countries," *Le
Nouvelliste,* May 3, 2016, https://lenouvelliste.com/article/156159/haitis-role-
in-the-independence-of-latin-american-countries

[255] Bynum, R., "Ga. monument dedicated to Haitian soldiers in American
Revolution," *Gwinnet Daily Post,* October 8, 2007, https://www.
gwinnettdailypost.com/archive/ga-monument-dedicated-to-haitian-soldiers-
in-american-revolution/article_1f7c9d2f-e0a8-51d8-805c-4dd1fb5c708e.
html#:~:text='We%20were%20here%20in%201779%20to%20help%20
America%20win%20independence.andtext=Though%20not%20well%20
known%20in,independence%20from%20France%20in%201804.

[256] Pierre, S. (Ed.) (2007). *Ces Québécois venus d'Haïti : Contribution de la
communauté haïtienne à l'édification du Québec moderne.* Montréal: Presses
inter Polytechnique.

[257] Bynum, 2016

[258] Semple, K., "'There is no hope': Crisis pushes Haiti to brink of collapse," *New
York Times,* October 20, 2019, https://www.nytimes.com/2019/10/20/world/
americas/Haiti-crisis-violence.html

[259] U.S. Department of Health and Human Services. (2020). Dietary Guidelines for Americans (8th Ed.). https://health.gov/our-work/food-and-nutrition/2015-2020-dietary-guidelines/

[260] Charles, J., "Why Has COVID Claimed Few Lives in Haiti Despite Lax Rules?"

[261] Such as Fisher, et al. (1982); and Hossain (2004)

[262] Fisher, et al., 1982, p. 27

[263] Popkin, 1990, p. 65

[264] Bandura cited in Popkin, 1990, p. 65

[265] Merriam-Webster. (2020). Work ethic. https://www.merriam-webster.com/dictionary/work%20ethic

[266] Stankovich, C. (2013). How perception impacts sports performance. https://drstankovich.com/how-perception-impacts-sports-performance/#:~:text=How%20we%20perceive%20things%20in,athletic%20potential%20as%20a%20result, para. 5

[267] Adelman, 2011, p. 92

[268] Kretzmann, J. P., and McKnight, J. L. (1993). *Building communities from the inside out: A path toward finding and mobilizing a community's assets.* Chicago, IL: ACTA Publications., p. 2

[269] Kretzmann and McKnight, 1993, p. 2

[270] Kretzmann and McKnight, 1993, p. 4

[271] Klarreich and Polman, 2012

[272] Kretzmann and McKnight, 1993, p. 4

[273] Klarreich and Polman, 2012

[274] Hammond, S. A. (2013). *The thin book of appreciative inquiry.* (3rd ed.). Plano, TX: Thin Book Pub., p. 14

[275] The World Bank, 2015, p. 58

[276] Schwartz, G. (2007). *When charity destroys dignity: Overcoming unhealthy dependency in the Christian movement.* Lancaster, PA: World Mission Associates., p. 14

[277] Corbett, S., and Fikkert, B. (2014). *When helping hurts: How to alleviate poverty without hurting the poor- and yourself.* Chicago: Moody Publishers., p. 118

[278] Corbett and Fikkert, 2009

[279] Linthicum, R. C. (2003). *Transforming power: Biblical strategies for making a difference in your community.* Downers Grove, IL: InterVarsity Press., p. 93; Schwartz, 2007; Corbett and Fikkert, 2009

[280] Klarreich and Polman, 2012

[281] Corbett and Fikkert, 2009, p. 119, p. 117

[282] The World Bank, 2015, p. 59

[283] Adelman, 2011, p. 93

[284] LaFranchi, H., "What helps Haiti? 'Working with' versus 'doing for,'" *Christian Science Monitor,* July 14, 2021, https://www.csmonitor.com/World/Americas/2021/0714/What-helps-Haiti-Working-with-versus-doing-for, para. 9

[285] ISPAN, 2020

[286] Henry Christophe quoted in ISPAN, 2020

[287] Corbett and Fikkert, 2009, p. 104

[288] Corbett and Fikkert, 2009, p. 104

[289] Gizelis, T. and Kosek, K. (2005). Why humanitarian interventions succeed or fail: The role of local participation. https://www.researchgate.net/publication/249715113_Why_Humanitarian_Interventions_Succeed_or_FailThe_Role_of_Local_Participation, p. 363

290 Ramachandran and Walz, 2015

291 Kretzmann and McKnight, 1993, p. 31

292 CIA, 2019

293 Emmaus University of Haiti; https://emmaus.edu.ht/

294 John F. Kennedy quoted in Wilkinson and Pickett, 2009, p. 103

295 Jadotte, 2008

296 Longley, R. (2019). Understanding the victim complex. https://www.thoughtco.com/victim-complex-4160276

297 Lexico. (2020). Reverse racism. https://www.lexico.com/definition/reverse_racism

298 Hand Up Micro-Credit; https://menleve.org/

299 Maslow, A. (1968). *Readings in the Economics of Education.* United Nations: UNESCO, p. 623

300 The World Bank, 2015

301 Adelman, 2011

302 Hand Up Micro-Credit; https://menleve.org/

303 Adelman, 2011, p. 92

304 Yunus, M. (2010). *Building social business: The new kind of capitalism that serves humanity's most pressing needs.* New York, NY: PublicAffairs, p.1

305 The World Bank. (2012). "What a Waste" Report Shows Alarming Rise in Amount, Costs of Garbage, https://www.worldbank.org/en/news/feature/2012/06/06/report-shows-alarming-rise-in-amount-costs-of-garbage

306 The World Bank Group. (2019). Climate change knowledge portal. https://climateknowledgeportal.worldbank.org/country/haiti/climate-data-historical

307 Kretzmann and McKnight, 1993, pp. 144-145

308 The World Bank, 2015

[309] Corbett and Fikkert, 2009, p. 94

[310] *Reach 4 Life.* (2004). Colorado Springs, CO: Biblica, Inc.

[311] Dictionary.com. (2020). Blessing. https://www.dictionary.com/browse/blessing#:~:text=a%20special%20favor%2C%20mercy%2C%20or,took%20turns%20reciting%20the%20blessing.

[312] Jewish Virtual Library (2020). Hebrew: Greetings and congratulations. https://www.jewishvirtuallibrary.org/hebrew-greetings-and-congratulations; See also Learn Religions. (2019). The meaning of As-Salamu Alaikum for Muslims. https://www.learnreligions.com/islamic-phrases-assalamu-alaikum-2004285

[313] Potter, 2006

[314] Wilkinson and Pickett, 2009, pp. 208-209

[315] Maggay, M. P. (2004). *Transforming society: reflections on the kingdom and politics.* Quezon City, Philippines: Institute for Studies in Asian Church and Culture. p. 33

[316] Maggay, 2004, p. 34

[317] Maggay, 2004, p. 32

[318] Maggay, 2004, p. 41

[319] Brueggemann, W. (2001). *The prophetic imagination.* Minneapolis, MN: Fortress Press, p. 17

[320] Brueggemann, 2001, p. 18

[321] Brueggemann, 2001, p. 15

[322] Brueggemann, 2001, p. 16

[323] Hammond, 2013, p. 24

[324] Merriam-Webster. (2020). Breakthrough. https://www.merriam-webster.com/dictionary/breakthrough

[325] Fanon, F. (1963). *The wretched of the earth.* New York: Grove Press.

[326] Rocke, K. and J. Van Dyke. (2012). *Geography of grace: Doing theology from below*. Tacoma, WA: Street Psalms Press. (Kindle 5), loc. 2492

[327] McNeil, B. and Richardson, R. (2009). *The Heart of Racial Justice: How Soul Change Leads to Social Change*. Downers Grove, Il: Intervarsity Press. (Kindle 5), loc. 676

[328] Wint, A. (2003). *Competitiveness in small developing economies*. Kingston, Jamaica: The University of the West Indies Press.

[329] Freire, 2000, p. 44

[330] Linthicum, 2003, p. 24

[331] Linthicum, 2003, p. 23

[332] Brueggemann, 2001

[333] Thomas, 2014

[334] Desmangles, 1992, p. 15

[335] Desmangles, 1992

[336] Thomas, 2014, p. 24

[337] Boers, T. and Stoner, T. (2012). *Demons of Poverty: One entrepreneur's experience with addressing poverty in Haiti*. Grand Rapids, MI: Acton Institute.

[338] Hiebert, 2008, p.118

[339] Maggay, M.P. (2019, June). Community Development. In Bakke Graduate University. City Immersion Overture. Lecture conducted from Manila, Philippines.

[340] Corbett and Fikkert, 2009, p. 88

[341] Boers and Stoner, 2012, p. 104

[342] Boers and Stoner, 2012, p. 105

[343] Harrison quoted in Boers and Stoner, 2012, p. 106

[344] Lucado, M. (2013). *God will carry you through*. Nashville, TN: Thomas Nelson, p. 174

[345] Lawless, R. (1992). *Haiti's bad press*. Rochester, Vt: Schenkman Books., p. 169

CPSIA information can be obtained
at www.ICGtesting.com
Printed in the USA
BVHW031209300323
661448BV00013B/550